A Word
from the Wise

A Word from the Wise

by
I. D. E. Thomas

MOODY PRESS
CHICAGO

The use of selected references from various versions of
the Bible in this publication does not necessarily imply
publisher endorsement of the versions in their entirety.

Library of Congress Cataloging in Publication Data

Thomas, Isaac David Ellis.
   A word from the wise.

   Includes bibliographical references.
    1. Bible. O.T. Proverbs—Criticism, interpretation, etc. I. Title.
BS1465.2.T45   223'.7'077   78-18803
ISBN 0-8024-9681-4

To my wife

Doubtless if the world were governed by the whole wisdom of this single Book, it would be 'a new earth, wherein dwelleth righteousness.'

CHARLES BRIDGES

Contents

1

SOLOMON AND HIS PROVERBS

There are thirty-one chapters in the book of Proverbs. A chapter for each day of the month! I believe that the wisdom of the book is such that it can equip a man to meet any problem that could possibly come his way.

Never before in history has man been so aware of his problems, and never before has he been so privileged to have those problems diagnosed and analyzed for him. There is no end to the scientific and technical expertise at his disposal. The market has a glut of consultants, all anxious to help him probe his inner psyche and bring him the relief and remedy needed. A man may choose to unwind and unravel his problems on a costly psychiatrist's couch, consult an astrologist for a private reading, or simply mail his problem direct to an Ann Landers or Abigail Van Buren for the price of a postage stamp.

The one abiding and unchanging element in the whole situation is the problems themselves. They remain basically the same as they have been from the beginning. "There is no new thing under the sun" was the verdict of Solomon (Ecclesiastes 1:9). A noted London lawyer said the same thing when he went on record recently and declared that there was no crime committed in modern-day London that could not be read of in the book of Genesis. Rudyard Kipling, trading poetry for prose, made a similar assertion half a century earlier:

> The craft that we call modern;
> The crimes that we call new;
> John Bunyan had 'em typed and filed,
> In 1682.

An important characteristic of the proverbs of Solomon is their practicality. They have only one aim: to equip us for the business of living. Whether our problems be personal, matrimonial, domestic, financial, spiritual, or general, the counsel of Proverbs is all-inclusive and abrasively relevant. Much of our modern-day preaching has been accused of being too speculative and hypothetical. Ministers have lost their people because of their preoccupation with philosophical and theological abstractions. As the British literary critic Hazlitt once said of poet S. T. Coleridge, "He had wings but wanted hands and feet." Solomon, however, can never be accused of indulging in abstractions, nor of leaving his readers suspended in midair. All his proverbs are "grounded." They apply to the very spot where the rubber hits the runway. Solomon tells it like it is.

At the same time, it should be added that although intensely practical, these proverbs also have theological content. They are not just plain, common sense, nor just plain wisdom. They are *from above.* Wisdom that is God-breathed. God is telling us through these proverbs what is required of us, and what are the incalculable blessings that result from their observance. It is no wonder that Jerome advised one of his friends, concerning the education of his daughter: "Let her have, first of all, the Book of Psalms for holiness of heart, and be instructed in the Proverbs of Solomon for the godly life."

SOLOMON

Sir Walter Scott rightly remarked that the question ought not only to be, *What* is said? but *Who* said it? Credibility depends as much on the character of the witness as on the nature of the evidence. What do we know about the human author of these proverbs? Who was he, and whence came he?

It is obvious, of course, that every verse in the book of Proverbs could not have come from the pen of Solomon. One section is attributed to Agur, and another to Lemuel. There are some sections that would seem to have been written *for* Solomon, and not *by* Solomon. However, I believe the major portion of the book belongs to Solomon; many of the proverbs could well have been selections from a much larger collection that Solomon wrote. In 1 Kings 4:32, we are told that his total collection came to three thousand proverbs, so it could well be that the proverbs found in the biblical book of Proverbs were culled from this larger group.

What do we know of Solomon? We know, of course, that his father was King David, and his mother, Bathsheba. We know that at his birth, the prophet Nathan called him Jedidiah, a name that meant "beloved of God," or "the divine darling"; but David, on instructions from God, called him Solomon, "the child of peace." After the strife and bloodshed of David's reign, his son would usher in a period of peace and tranquillity for the people of Israel.

Solomon succeeded his father to the throne and became the last king to reign over a united Israel. After his day, ten of the tribes went their own way under Jeroboam, and only two tribes remained loyal to Solomon's son and heir, Rehoboam.

DISTINCTIVE FEATURES OF SOLOMON'S REIGN

It was first, as already suggested, a reign of peace. The people enjoyed a peace and tranquillity so different from the storms and turbulence of the days of David. It is said that when Solomon built the Temple, he used only the minimum amount of iron because iron, according to his prophets, was a metal of war.

It was not all peace, however, especially in the early years of his reign. Being anxious to establish himself securely on the throne, Solomon did what many other kings had done: he set about eliminating his rivals. He killed Adonijah, his brother, and Joab, the military commander of his father's forces. He also deposed Abiathar from the high priesthood and appointed Zadok in his place. It soon became obvious to all in Israel that it was advantageous to be in the good graces of the new king. "The king's wrath," said Solomon, "is as the roaring of a lion; but his favour is as dew upon the grass" (Proverbs 19:12).

It was a reign of effective administration. Solomon abolished the old boundaries between the twelve tribes, and by so doing minimized tribal consciousness and encouraged national unity. He then divided the country into twelve new geographical districts, each under a governor, with each governor answerable to Solomon. In this way, the administrative affairs of the country were vastly improved; justice was better administered, and soon law and order prevailed from Dan to Beersheba.

It was a reign of great prosperity. Solomon encouraged foreign commerce and made trade agreements with many lands. He imported gold, silver, precious stones, and ivory into Israel; Solomon himself

lived in a gold-plated palace with all the extrava-
gances of lavishness and luxury. We are told that his
tableware was of solid gold and that he exceeded all
the kings of the earth in riches. His annual income
was approximately six hundred and sixty-six talents
of gold—a figure in excess of $20 million. Foreign
dignitaries were overwhelmed by the grandeur and
glory of his kingdom, and commented on the magnifi-
cence of his life-style. Even the details were not over-
looked: the gourmet food, the livery of the attendants,
the tapestries, and so on.

It was a reign of magnificent construction. It
seems that Solomon had a passion for building programs. Beautifying Jerusalem became one of his life's
ambitions. He built a magnificent royal palace for
himself—a task that took thirteen years to accomplish;
a number of cedarwood palaces for his wives, and a
host of other magnificent buildings. In fact, he put the
little Judean city of Jerusalem on a par with Tyre,
Sidon, and Rameses.

His most noteworthy accomplishment, however,
was the Temple on Mount Moriah. It had been the desire of David, his father, to build this Temple, but God
forbade a man who had shed so much blood to build
the Temple of peace. It is to David's credit, however,
that rather than feel sorry for himself and do nothing,
he saw to it that the materials for the building were all
gathered and prepared beforehand. So, on the death of
David, Solomon was able to proceed without delay
with the task of construction. He imported skilled
craftsmen from Phoenicia to aid him. It was a superb
undertaking, and when completed, the Temple domi-
nated the skyline of the eternal city. It was, in the
words of Lewis Browne, "infinitely the most significant building ever erected by the hands of man."

Even more important than the masonry and architecture was the fact that this building became the earthly locale of the divine Shekinah. It was the place where God was pleased to meet His people. At times Solomon's enemies would maliciously ask, "Was it not the son of Bathsheba who built the temple?" But God overruled all such remarks and sanctioned the Shekinah glory to descend and rest on this holy building.

Solomon's outstanding personal feature, however, was his great wisdom and understanding. His was no ordinary human talent, but a special gift bestowed upon him by God. After the day of the thousand offerings at Gibeon, Solomon made the noblest choice that mortal man could ever make. He asked God for "an understanding heart." That pleased the Lord, and He told Solomon, "Because thou hast asked this thing, and hast not asked for thyself long life; neither hast asked riches for thyself, nor hast asked the life of thine enemies . . . behold, I have done according to thy words: lo, I have given thee a wise and an understanding heart; so that there was none like thee before thee, neither after thee shall any arise like unto thee. And I have also given thee that which thou hast not asked, both riches, and honour" (1 Kings 3:11-13). These promises were all fulfilled.

Some years after that event at Gibeon, a royal dignitary was to travel from the uttermost parts of the earth to see and hear for herself the wisdom of this man Solomon. She was the famed Queen of Sheba. She had already heard of his wisdom back home in Sheba, but what she heard from his own lips in Jerusalem made her exclaim: "The half was not told me" (1 Kings 10:7).

ILLUSTRATIONS OF SOLOMON'S WISDOM

The Bible supplies us with one noted example of Solomon's judicial wisdom. Two harlots sought his judgment as to which one was the rightful mother of a child. It seems each woman had given birth to a child, three days apart. One mother, however, had lain on top of her child while she was asleep, and the child had died. She had then substituted her dead child for the living child while the other woman was asleep. In the morning, on awakening, this other woman discovered that the child in her bosom was dead, and what was more, that it was not her child. She guessed what had happened and demanded the return of her own child. The dispute went to arbitration, and finally to the king himself. The Bible tells us what happened:

> And the king said, Bring me a sword. . . . Divide the living child in two, and give half to the one, and half to the other. Then spake the woman whose the living child was unto the king, for her bowels yearned upon her son, and she said, O my lord, give her the living child, and in no wise slay it. But the other said, Let it be neither mine nor thine, but divide it. Then the king answered and said, Give her the living child, and in no wise slay it: she is the mother thereof (1 Kings 3:24-27).

A similar example of Solomon's judicial wisdom is found in the story of the three brothers. It is different from the first example in that it comes to us from an extrabiblical source, but it conveys the same trait in the character of Solomon and the same shrewdness of judgment.

> One day three brothers came before him. Their father, they said, had died on the previous day. Just before his death he had told them that he was leaving all his possessions to his only legitimate son. And now each one of them claimed that he, and he alone, was the one legitimate son.
> King Solomon heard their story and sat back and pondered. How was he to determine the true son and heir? Finally he turned to them.

"Let the body of your dead father be brought here, and let it be placed upright against a pillar."

The brothers did as they were ordered.

"And now," said the king, "bring me a bow and three arrows."

When the bow and the arrows had been brought, King Solomon commanded each one of the three brothers to shoot an arrow at the dead man. "He whose aim is the best shall be adjudged the true heir."

The eldest of the three brothers took careful aim and pierced the dead man in the arm.

"Well done," said the king.

The aim of the second brother was better. He succeeded in piercing the dead man's forehead.

"Very well done!" observed Solomon.

The youngest brother took aim and then threw the bow and arrow upon the ground. "I would rather lose my inheritance than desecrate my father's body."

"You," exclaimed King Solomon, "are the true heir!"

One more illustration, again from an extrabiblical source, will show the ingenious methods that Solomon pursued to arrive at the right judgment.

One day he [Solomon] called to him an officer who was reputed to be the most faithful man in Jerusalem. "If you fulfill my orders," said the king, "I will honor you."

The man bowed low. "His Majesty commands, his subjects obey. What is His Majesty's will?"

"Take this sword," said the king, "and if tomorrow morning you bring me the head of your wife, I will make you governor over all my other governors."

The man took the sword and returned the next day—but without his wife's head. "I drew the blade," he said, "when my wife was asleep. But, as I was about to strike, I noticed how her hair was spread over the pillow and fell upon the faces of our two children. I couldn't bring myself to do it."

The next day Solomon called this man's wife, who

was reputed to be the most faithful woman in Jerusalem. "Take this sword," he said to her. "And if tomorrow you bring me the head of your husband, I will make you my queen."

The woman took the sword and went home. That night she prepared a banquet for her husband. And, as soon as he fell into a heavy sleep from the fumes of the wine, she brought the sword sharply down upon his neck. But Solomon in his wisdom had given her a sword of tin. The blow awakened the husband but did him no harm.[1]

PROVERBS

Proverbs were plentiful in ancient times, particularly in the lands bordering the Mediterranean. Countries like Egypt, Greece, and Persia boasted of their collections of wise sayings, and Solomon was undoubtedly acquainted with all of them. The land of Israel also had its wise sayings, and many of them were incorporated into the Hebrew Scriptures.

What exactly is a proverb? The features of a proverb might be defined as shortness, sense, and salt! A proverb's function, according to one author, is to prick, penetrate, and probe.

The American College Dictionary definition is: "A short, popular saying . . . embodying some familiar truth . . . in expressive language."

The word *proverb* as used in ordinary parlance would have two distinctive features: (a) wisdom or truth as content; and (b) conciseness in form. It is wisdom distilled into a short, succinct sentence, thus making it memorable and effective.

The very conciseness of a proverb adds to its incisiveness. Because of this, a proverb often hits the mark before a man has time to raise his defenses. When he fully realizes what has happened, it is too late to stop it. Just as Alexander Whyte said of Nathan's censure of David: "Nathan's sword was within an inch of David's conscience before David knew that Nathan had a sword. One sudden thrust and the king was at Nathan's feet."

In the Bible, however, the word *proverb* (Hebrew, *Mashal*) has a much broader connotation than the modern use of the word. In some instances it would seem to have no essential difference from the word *parable*. It is also used to describe a prophecy like that of Balaam in Numbers 23-24; a didactic poem like that found in Job 27:1; and a satirical statement like the one in Isaiah 14:4. Sometimes the word refers to dark sayings, riddles, puzzles, and intricate questions, all of which were fascinating to the Oriental mind.

It is claimed that the root meaning of the word in Hebrew implies "to rule," thus carrying with it a note of authority. If we take this meaning, we may then interpret the book of Proverbs as a sort of manual of terse, authoritative sayings, containing rules and guidelines for godly living. They are not merely human rules, but rules that are God-given and God-breathed, and carry God's own imprimatur. And, like the rest of Scripture, their purpose is to make the man of God perfect and "[thoroughly] furnished unto all good works" (2 Timothy 3:17).

DISTINCTIVE FEATURES OF SOLOMON'S PROVERBS

They are based on observation. Solomon anticipated the empirical method of our day: he observed events around him and made the right deductions. He was a student both of nature and of human nature, and during his lifetime he accumulated a vast reservoir of knowledge. He has been acclaimed as one of the most illustrious men in history, a man of large mind and inquiring spirit. His fame was widespread even in his own day. The Bible states that his "wisdom excelled the wisdom of all the children of the east country, and all the wisdom of Egypt. For he was wiser than all men . . . and his fame was in all nations round about" (1 Kings 4:30-31).

Solomon's observations encompassed the field of *economics*, for he was the man who made little Israel the economic envy of the nations. He traded in gold, silver, ivory, and armor: "The king made silver to be in Jerusalem as stones, and cedars made he to be as the sycamore" (1 Kings 10:27). He engaged in *botanical research*. He wrote treatises on plant life: "from the cedar tree that is in Lebanon even unto the hyssop that springeth out of the wall" (1 Kings 4:33). *Biology* could well be added to the list of his interests: "he spake also of beasts, and of fowl, and of creeping things, and of fishes" (1 Kings 4:33). Like his father, Solomon also engaged in *literary* pursuits, excelling in psalms and proverbs. From all these observations and interests, he distilled for us the abiding essence of great wisdom.

They are drawn from personal experience. Solomon's proverbs contain infinitely more than abstract philosophy or hypothetical theory; they contain wisdom gleaned and garnered from the events of his own life. In his formative years, Solomon had as his guide and mentor the prophet Nathan, and no doubt received much instruction from him. But the proverbs Solomon penned contain more than instruction received from others: they are charged with actual experiences. The things he wrote about were the things he himself had known. We are given the impression that they were written down *after*, not *before*, the event—hindsight, not foresight. Rather than enter his library to weave subtle and ingenious formulas, Solomon consulted his records and diaries and drew the appropriate lessons. His proverbs were manufactured

in the crucible of personal experience, the heat of
daily conduct and conflict. When Solomon spoke of
sin and its inevitable retribution, it was not only as a
general, universal law but as something that happened to him and seared his soul in the process.
When he spoke of the fear of the Lord as the beginning of knowledge, he was silently confessing the
vanity of all other philosophies, which he had at one
time tried and found wanting. When he told us, "It is
better to dwell in the wilderness, than with a conten-
tious and an angry woman" (Proverbs 21:19), he may
well have been recalling his own misery, experienced
at the hands of his numerous, alien wives. It was from
his own foolishnesses that he mined some of his choicest nuggets of wisdom.

They are inbreathed by a divine relationship.
Solomon's relationship with and dependence upon
God provide the clues to his distinctiveness and real
greatness. Solomon not only observed for himself, but
he also readily acknowledged that God was the source
and giver of his wisdom. His was no mere human trait
cultivated carefully over the years and based only on
human observation and experience, but a special gift
bestowed upon him by a specific act of God. It should
be remembered that the man who composed these
proverbs also composed prayers; the man who built
palaces also built a Temple; the man who administered the law of the land also upheld the Law of God.
It was that distinctive relationship with and reliance
upon God that made his proverbs immortal. In the ultimate sense, these proverbs came not from Solomon
at all, but from Solomon's God. "The pen is that of the
King of Israel; but the words are wisdom of God"
(Charles Bridges).

There is one more thing that should be said: the
wisdom found in Proverbs seems at times to assume

personality. It takes on human form. "Wisdom *crieth* without; she *uttereth* her voice in the streets: she *crieth* in the chief place of concourse, in the openings of the gates" (Proverbs 1:20-21, emphasis added). In these and other verses, wisdom seems to become personified and incarnate—she cries and speaks and commands. We know, of course, that the actual incarnation of wisdom did not occur for another one thousand years. It was then, in the fullness of time, that the one greater than Solomon appeared who was in truth the Logos and Wisdom of God.

A SAD POSTSCRIPT

The question is inevitable: Did Solomon heed his own wisdom? Did he practice his own instruction? The answer, unfortunately, has to be in the negative. It became a national tragedy that this exceedingly wise man, whose proverbs have been an inspiration to countless millions, failed to practice his own teaching. As a matter of fact, his life ended on a dark and somber note. The tragedy was compounded by the exceptional advantages this man had enjoyed: great wisdom, unlimited resources, absolute power, endless opportunities, a mighty kingdom, and a peaceful reign. In the words of the inimitable Alexander Whyte:

> If ever there was a shining type of Christ in the Old Testament church, it was Solomon. If ever any one was once enlightened, and had tasted the heavenly gift, and was made a partaker of the Holy Ghost, and had tasted the good word of God, and the powers of the world to come, it was Solomon. If ever any young saint sought first the kingdom of God and His righteousness, and had all these things added unto him, it was Solomon.[2]

Yet his life, which had opened in a blaze of glory, ended in deep cynicism and dark despair. His surfeit of pleasures became ashes in his mouth. His own confession was: "All is vanity and vexation of spirit" (Ecclesiastes 1:14b). It is no wonder that Solomon has been called the greatest castaway in the Bible.

What accounted for such a tragic situation? How did it happen? It can be explained best in terms of the Law of God. In Deuteronomy 17:16-17, God explicitly stated that the king of Israel should avoid three particular pitfalls: multiplying horses, multiplying wives, and multiplying wealth. Solomon failed in all three.

Solomon built strong military forces of chariots and horses, and then deposited his faith in them rather than God. He boasted of "a thousand and four hundred chariots, and twelve thousand horsemen" (1 Kings 10:26).

Solomon followed the custom of other Eastern potentates and established a harem of wives and concubines, even choosing his own queen from Pharaoh's court in Egypt (1 Kings 11:1-3).

Solomon also accumulated great riches and developed an extravagant appetite for luxuries (1 Kings 10:27). In 1 Kings 10:22, we are told that once every three years the navy of Tharshish would bring him gold, silver, ivory, and apes.

An interesting side question is why the navy should bring Solomon apes. And should they be listed alongside gold, silver, and ivory? In this again, Solomon was indicating that God was not his security. It was the custom of many Eastern monarchs to use apes to guard their palaces. The apes were thoroughly trained and could be depended upon to act in accordance with their training. In many ways they were more dependable and loyal than human guards: apes would never indulge in intrigue and insurrection. So Solomon removed himself from the protection of God, and even from that of men, and trusted his physical security to a contingent of apes.

Solomon's religion, which originally had been so pure and clean, became tainted. To please his alien wives, he allowed their idols and cults to be introduced into Jerusalem in a sort of ecumenical bonhomie. The separated life was not for Solomon. Soundness of belief and purity of behavior became unimportant. "For it came to pass, when Solomon was old, that his wives turned away his heart after other gods: and his heart was not perfect with the LORD his God, as was the heart of David his father" (1 Kings 11:4). Having accommodated his faith to that of his alien wives, he next indulged in their debaucheries and dissipations. The unrivaled purveyor of wisdom became a dissolute Eastern monarch. It is significant that the man who succeeded him on the throne, the unwise Rehoboam, was a son of one of these alien women, Naamah the Ammonitess (1 Kings 14:21, 31).

The most tragic element of all, however, is that as we scrutinize the details of his life and death, we find no reference anywhere to contrition of heart or repentance of spirit. There is no note of regret, no tear of penitence. It is in this respect that he differs most greatly from his father, David. In vain do we search the songs and proverbs of Solomon for anything that approximates Psalm 51. We find remorse, yes; but repentance, no. Whereas David could say, "Create in me a clean heart, O God; and renew a right spirit within me" (Psalm 51:10), the best that Solomon could say was, "Even in laughter the heart is sorrowful; and the end of that mirth is heaviness" (Proverbs 14:13). Or, in the words of a modern paraphrase: "Laughter cannot mask a heavy heart. When the laughter ends, the grief remains" (TLB).

Proverbs 3:1-2
My Son, forget not my law;
but let thine heart keep my commandments:
For length of days, and long life,
and peace, shall they add to thee.

2

HOW TO LIVE LONGER?

The British magazine *Punch* carried a cartoon some years ago in which a little boy was asking his father: "Dad, what did you do in the last war?"

To which his dad replied: "Well . . . I survived."

The instinct to survive is deeply ingrained in our nature, and man will pay any price and make any sacrifice just to live a little longer. It is this promise of longevity that is offered here in the book of Proverbs. It is made to those who keep the law of God and observe His commandments.

In the opinion of many people, such a promise is questionable. To some, it is simply not true. Not only do the good die young, but saints die young also. History supplies a thousand examples, from Henry Martyn to Nate Saint. Jesus Himself only lived thirty-three years. To others, even if the promise is true, it is an unworthy one. It betrays self-interest and reduces Christianity to the level of an insurance policy: accept Christ and obey His commandments, and you will live to an old age! In the opinion of these people, such an approach degrades the Bible, making it no better than a "How to Look Younger and Live Longer" manual.

There is no doubt, of course, that the promise of

25

longevity is highly popular. Indeed, could anything
be more popular?

The science of gerontology has assumed great
importance in our time, and anything that can reverse
the process of aging and add to our life span has no
scarcity of patrons. There are research centers around
the world engaged in the effort to overcome aging
and, according to some, death itself. Such is the
rodomontade of men that they consider death to be an
imposition and physical immortality a human possibility. Pierre Auger, the French physicist, has told us
that death "may be a manipulable genetic character."
Shades of John Strachey in the prewar years!
Strachey had such faith in human omnipotence that
he predicted the day when man would attain "terres-
trial immortality." Not a case of living forever in the
next world, but in this world! But poor John Strachey:
a few years later and he, too, went the way of all flesh.
Others believe in the practice of anabiosis, a process
in which the body is immediately frozen at death, and
kept in that condition until some future date when it
can be revived. All these efforts point to the fact that
life is sweet. Who wants to die? No wonder Queen
Elizabeth I said on her deathbed, "All my possessions
for one moment of time."

Is this promise of longevity a worthy motive by
which to woo men and women to God and a life of
righteousness? Is Solomon lowering the standard in
order to appeal to man's baser instincts? There are two
questions we have to answer: (a) Is the promise of
longevity worthy? (b) Is the promise of longevity factual?

The answer to the first question is much easier
than the answer to the second question. Whereas
goodness does bring its reward, we are not taught to
be good merely for the sake of the reward. If that were

the case, we would not be good but simply self-seeking. Longevity is the *reward* of goodness, but it should never be the *cause* of goodness.

Before we proceed to answer the second question about whether the promise of longevity is factual, let us note exactly what Solomon says in this context. "My son, forget not my law; but let thine heart keep my commandments: for length of days, and long life, and peace, shall they add to thee" (Proverbs 3:1-2). That is the promise, and it is repeated many times over in the book of Proverbs. You find it, among other places, in Proverbs 3:16; 4:10; 9:11; and 10:27. Outside the book of Proverbs, you find it repeated in a number of other biblical passages. An example would be Exodus 20:12: "Honour thy father and thy mother: that thy days may be long upon the land which the LORD thy God giveth thee."

Regretfully, a little bit of demolition is necessary here before expounding on the meaning of this promise. All agree that longevity is a promise made specifically to the righteous. The problem, however, is this: all the righteous do not see the fulfillment of this promise. In other words, some of them do not live a long life, but are cut down in middle age, and even in youth.

Some commentators have attempted to get around the difficulty by giving the term *longevity* an atypical interpretation. Even the great Bridges did this. He said in his *An Exposition of Proverbs* that longevity "as regards this life has no charm. To the ungodly it is a curse; to the people of God a trial of faith and patience; to all a weariness." That being the case, he seems to imply that the blessing of longevity must be interpreted in terms of the next life. The promise made here in the proverbs of Solomon, however, is decidedly referring to *this* life. The Hebrew phrase lit-

erally means "extension of days." It is a phrase limited to the present stage of existence, to this world,
and should be interpreted as such. Longevity in the
next world, whether it be in heaven or in hell, is
meaningless. Longevity makes no sense in the context
of eternity. Eternity cannot be added unto or sub-
tracted from. Longevity is obviously a term of time.
Therefore, the promise made here by Solomon has to
be understood in terms of this present world.

To further substantiate the point, the Bible states
that in contrast to the longevity of the righteous, the
wicked will be cut down early, and the number of
their days will be shortened.

Only in this sense can this promise be understood: the days of the righteous will be lengthened,
and the days of the unrighteous will be shortened,
here in this present world.

This being so, how then is the promise to be interpreted, especially in view of the fact that many of
the righteous die young? Clearly, the promise should
be interpreted in general terms. The principle em-
bodied in the promise can only be understood as a
general one, and as such it allows many exceptions.
The general principle is—and this can be stated
unequivocally—that the righteous will outlive the unrighteous. In other words, God declares that normally
and generally the virtuous life will add to a man's
years. Goodness, honesty, integrity, purity, and love
will lengthen a man's days. On the other hand, all sin,
wickedness, corruption, debauchery, and dissoluteness will shorten a man's days. It is true that there are
exceptions, but as a general principle there is not the
least doubt that the promise is true.

Joseph Parker meant the same thing, although he
expressed it a little differently, when he said that this
promise of longevity must be understood in *ideal*

terms. And he added a felicitous note when he said, "Ideality is often the true reality." So by interpreting Solomon's words in an ideal or general sense, we believe we have the meaning that Solomon intended. Ideally and generally, the godly life does lead to longevity, and the sinful life does lead to an early demise. Whether he be conscious of it or not, or whether he likes it or not, the sinner is casting his vote for a short life. By his debauchery and dissipation he is forfeiting the gift of longevity.

FORFEITING LONGEVITY

Some forfeit longevity consciously. They decide to shorten their days by deliberate choice. We can be happy that these are few in number; but unfortunately, the number is on the increase. This is especially true among the youth of our nation. During the past twenty years the rate of suicide among young people between the ages of fifteen and twenty-five has gone up more than 250 percent. On college campuses, suicide has become the number-two cause of death, surpassed only by accidents. Psychoanalyst Herbert Hendin has a chapter on student suicide that he entitled "Growing Up Dead" in his book *The Age of Sensation*. He puts the major blame for student suicide on the students' parents. In a recent interview he stated: "Today much more than twenty years ago, people are more egocentric, more interested in their own gratifications and satisfactions. They don't want to sacrifice. Before, they were willing to sacrifice too much perhaps. Now it is too little. Today there is a sense that anything that doesn't do things for them is resented. Children are seen as a burden. More and more parents are not finding them a source of joy or pleasure." He summarized the problem: "A lot of kids sense that they are the source of their parents' unhappiness. They sense that their parents feel trapped by marriage and that they are the lid on the trap. . . . Out of the tragic disaffection has come the rising number of young people who are drawn to suicide because 'deadness' has been their only security for a lifetime."

Sigmund Freud, the noted psychoanalyst, taught that there are two great forces, or basic instincts, in life. One he called the death wish (Thanatos), and the other the life wish (Eros). There are many psychiatrists who teach that the death wish is the stronger of the two.

It may be significant that psychiatrists themselves commit suicide at a rate four times that of the general public. Of Freud's own original cloister of twelve satellite psychiatrists, no less than seven committed suicide. As already made clear, it cannot be claimed that suicide is a matter of ignorance, since so many psychiatrists and so many of our educated youth choose it as a way out. Nor can it be claimed that suicide is a matter of poverty; as a matter of fact, suicide statistics in both the United States and the United Kingdom reveal that the percentage of rich people who commit suicide is eight times higher than the percentage of poor people who commit suicide. Nor does it seem to be a matter of being a loser in life and failing to make the grade: Hannibal made the grade, and so did Van Gogh, Freddy Mills, Marilyn Monroe, Ernest Hemingway, and Vicky the cartoonist. Klaus Mann (son of novelist Thomas Mann) stated: "I have lost more friends through suicide than through diseases, crimes, or accidents." And it does not surprise us to learn that far more of those who indulge in the so-called good-time life commit suicide than do those who live on the drab fringes of society.

It has been well said that it is not a question of what you learn, nor of what you earn, nor of what you

burn! The people named above, like King Saul of Israel, had all the advantages that life could offer:
wealth, fame, power, and pleasure. But also, like Saul,
they discovered that tinsel brings no satisfaction.
What good is a crown, a throne, or a scepter if there is
a void in the heart?

How true it is that men can multiply palaces but
have no homes; multiply wives but have no love;
multiply acquaintances but have no friends; multiply
pleasures but have no joy; multiply things but have
nothing. Nothing, that is, but an early grave and a lost
eternity.

> I tried the broken cisterns, Lord,
>   But, ah! the waters failed;
> E'en as I stooped to drink they fled,
>   And mocked me as I wailed.

Some people forfeit longevity subconsciously.
Although they would never consciously choose death,
they choose a life-style that can only accelerate death.
They do not sit down to reason through the issue and
then deliberately choose death; they simply indulge in
habits and excesses that can only hasten death. They
refuse to face the fact that there is a direct link between their dissipation and an early grave. Suicide by
installments! They will not face this fact for the simple reason that they do not want to face it. They prefer
to eliminate all such unpleasant thinking from their
conscious minds. All they suceed in doing, however,
is to bury it deeper. They submerge it in their subconscious minds, where it remains hidden.

In spite of their efforts, however, there do come
moments when such thoughts refuse to lie dormant
and insist on surfacing and reentering consciousness.
At such times they are forced to think about it again
and recognize its validity. But as soon as they can

they will push it back down, hoping for another re-
prieve. The chain smoker is aware of the link with
cancer—statistics make the fact very clear to him. The
alcoholic is aware of the link with cirrhosis of the
liver; the drug addict of the link with damaged brain
tissue; and the dissolute of the link with venereal
epidemics. Yet such cursed thoughts are pushed back
into the subconscious, as quickly and as deeply as
possible. To them, life's greatest remedy is forgetful-
ness. After all, if you do not want to do anything
about it, it is better not to think about it. And who
wants to think about sin and death?

In the 1950s, a lot was heard of the beatnick generation, "the bearded followers of Sartre." Haight-
Ashbury, a San Francisco neighborhood, or district,
became their national sanctuary. A few years ago, a
study was made of fifty-one hard-core members of this
beatnick generation to ascertain what had become of
them in the intervening years. A number of surprising
facts came to light. It was discovered that some were
already dead; some had returned to the "square" life;
some were living in "Bohemian" conditions; some
were drifting like zombies around San Francisco,
flinching and twitching and blankfaced; but the vast
majority were in mental institutions, unable to face
reality. They had learned their lesson too late: "God is
not mocked: for whatsoever a man soweth, that shall
he also reap" (Galatians 6:7).

"Excessive worldliness," said Charles Bridges,
"wears out the spring of life."

Other people will forfeit longevity unconsciously.
These people are unaware of the link between a life of
sin and an early grave for the simple reason that no
one told them. Obviously, as far as this country is
concerned, there are very few in this category. But
even for those, ignorance is no defense. As in the case

of law, so in the case of life: ignorance does not acquit. The dissolute and debauched life leads to an early death whether one is aware of it or not. No doubt a scriptural case could be made that would diminish the responsibility of such people, and this we accept. The Scriptures do teach that "unto whomsoever much is given, of him shall be much required" (Luke 12:48). And conversely, to whom little is given, little is required. Whatever the responsibility of such people is, the consequences remain the same. Whether a man is knowledgeable or ignorant, informed or uninformed, he still reaps the same results. Sin is no respecter of persons.

LONGER THAN LONG

If the Lord should condescend to bestow upon us this gift of longevity, it is still advisable to remember one thing: one day the gift will be exhausted. One day we, too, will die. In the words of Karl Menninger, "Death is ultimately sovereign—it wins." So the gift of longevity, provided we receive it, is still a limited gift. Whether it be for seventy, eighty, ninety, or one hundred years, it is still limited.

But as every Christian knows, there is a gift that is unlimited, and of far greater importance than longevity. This is the gift of everlasting life in Jesus Christ. There is no denying the factuality of this gift; and what is more, it is a gift that need not be interpreted in general or ideal terms. It is a specific and concrete gift; a gift that carries the imprimatur of God; a gift established in the heavens, and recorded in the Word. It is the reason Jesus came to this world, "that they might have life" (John 10:10). Here is the gift of all gifts: God's gift of eternal life to the believer.

Here is another truth well worth our consideration: at the time when our physical life is decaying on the way to the grave, our spiritual life is "renewed day by day" (2 Corinthians 4:16). Still another truth—one that concerns our final destiny: sin will not only shorten physical life, but more importantly, it will deprive us of eternal life. The verdict of Scripture is clear: "The soul that sinneth, it shall die" (Ezekiel 18:4b). And Solomon underscored the same verdict when he said: "He that sinneth against me wrongeth his own soul: all they that hate me love death" (Proverbs 8:36).

This is the choice before us, expressed in succinct but sure terms: sin and die, or believe and live. It is the same choice that was before the people of Israel three thousand years ago: "See, I have set before thee this day life and good, and death and evil" (Deuteronomy 30:15). "Choose you this day" (Joshua 24:15).

Proverbs 5:3-23

For the lips of a strange woman drop as an hon-
eycomb, and her mouth is smoother than oil: but her
end is bitter as wormwood, sharp as a twoedged
sword. Her feet go down to death; her steps take hold
on hell. Lest thou shouldest ponder the path of life,
her ways are moveable, that thou canst not know
them. Hear me now therefore, O ye children, and de-
part not from the words of my mouth. Remove thy way
far from her, and come not nigh the door of her house:
lest thou give thine honour unto others, and thy years
unto the cruel: lest strangers be filled with thy wealth;
and thy labours be in the house of a stranger; and
thou mourn at the last, when thy flesh and thy body
are consumed, and say, How have I hated instruction,
and my heart despised reproof; and have not obeyed
the voice of my teachers, nor inclined mine ear to
them that instructed me! I was almost in all evil in the
midst of the congregation and assembly. Drink waters
out of thine own cistern, and running waters out of
thine own well. Let thy fountains be dispersed abroad,
and rivers of waters in the streets. Let them be only
thine own, and not strangers' with thee. Let thy foun-
tain be blessed: and rejoice with the wife of thy youth.
Let her be as the loving hind and pleasant roe; let her
breasts satisfy thee at all times; and be thou ravished
always with her love. And why wilt thou, my son, be
ravished with a strange woman, and embrace the
bosom of a stranger? For the ways of man are before
the eyes of the LORD, and he pondereth all his goings.
His own iniquities shall take the wicked himself, and
he shall be holden with the cords of his sins. He shall
die without instruction; and in the greatness of his
folly he shall go astray.

3

SEX BETWEEN CONSENTING ADULTS?

A question frequently asked these days is whether sexual sins are all that serious. When two consenting adults engage in a sexual experience with no victim involved, is that to be considered a serious breach of the moral law of God?

Let us begin by making an all-too-obvious statement: sin is not limited to sex. Nor is sin limited to the flesh. There are "spiritual" sins, which in most cases are more serious and more lasting. Normally, although not invariably, sins of the flesh will decrease with age, whereas sins of the spirit will increase with age. The spirit belongs to an eternal order, so that sins of the spirit are often accentuated by the process of time. Let us look at a few examples.

SPIRITUAL SINS

There is the spiritual sin of *covetousness*. It is what the Puritan Thomas Watson would call "dry drunkenness." In the great literature of the world, practically without exception, the miser is depicted as an old man, shriveled with age; never a young man with the blush of spring upon his cheeks, but an old

37

man of furrowed brow, hoary head, and tottering
footstep. There he stands on the edge of the grave, and
one of his last acts before finally entering into it is to
count and recount his hoarded shekels. As Shakespeare told us in *Henry IV*, "A man can no more separate
age and covetousness, than 'a can part young limbs."

Take a look into your own heart and ask whether
this is not true. Is not materialism a greater temptation
in your life today than it was ten years ago? Do not the
paycheck and the bank account mean much more
today than they did when you were a youth of
twenty? As we age we have a tendency to substitute
gold for God.

Then there is the sin of *pride*. It is not the young
woman but the old woman who emerges as the incarnation of pride. Study her life and you will find that
snobbishness and arrogance have matured with the
years. She will insist on her say, demand her way, and
cling to her proud habits with grit and determination.
Cross an old woman whose pride has grown over the
years and you will find a Jezebel.

Much as we hear about the sins of youth, they are
no match for the sins of age. The saints of God are the
first to admit this fact. That is why you will find them
praying to their dying hour for grace not to disgrace
their Lord. One of the last prayers of saintly old
George Muller was for God to keep him from de-
veloping into a wicked old man!

SEXUAL SINS

We can never minimize spiritual sins, and it is
worthwhile to recall that Jesus reserved some of His
sternest rebukes for such sins. To state this, however,
does not in the least excuse us from other sins—the
sins of the flesh and, specifically, the sins of sex. Jesus
condemned them as well. There is no way we can

deny their seriousness or disregard the unmitigated suffering that results from them. Anything that defiles the body defiles the temple of the Holy Spirit and thereby merits the indignation and punishment of almighty God. According to Scripture, God will not reckon him guiltless who breaks His moral law in terms of sex. Sexual sins are serious sins, serious enough to keep a man out of the Kingdom of God. Do not be hoodwinked by the permissive, playboy philosophies of our day; sexual sins are hell-deserving sins.

Solomon deals with this question in Proverbs, chapter 5. It is a chapter that has the ring of experience. Solomon knew of what he was writing. Verification, if needed, can be found in 1 Kings 11:1-8 and Ecclesiastes 7:26. The "strange woman" that he referred to in this chapter of Proverbs could mean one of two things: a loose-living woman of easy virtue, or an alien woman—that is, a non-Israelite woman. Or, of course, it could mean both: in that case, the sin would be doubly repugnant because it transgressed both God's law regarding purity and God's law regarding separation. For our study, we shall interpret the word to mean that the strange woman of whom Solomon was writing was a woman of loose sexual morals, a woman guilty of promiscuous behavior, and skilled in the art of seduction.

Before we proceed, let it be made clear that although Solomon depicted woman as the seductress here, he was not suggesting that woman has a monopoly on this sin. The male is equally guilty—often more so. He, too, knows the tricks of the seducer's trade and will not hesitate to use them to gratify his lust. Solomon, however, chose here to paint seduction in the guise of a woman. He was, no doubt, drawing from material with which he was personally acquainted. He was also personally acquainted with the pain and anguish that come from such associations. His words have the ring of authenticity as he warns young men everywhere to cease all contact with such women. He was not writing from the standpoint of a man living in elevated heights beyond the reach of seduction, but of a man "of like passions as we are." He, too, knew of the lust that burns within us, and of the fires that blaze in our mortal frames. He knew all this, and he also knew how useless are the attempts of man to extinguish them. He knew that civilization and education can exercise a cushioning effect on human behavior and can, at times, subdue some of the more beastial and primitive instincts within us. But he also knew that they can never hope to deliver us from them. They can keep them submerged for a while, but conquer them—never! Once the restraints are removed, the sinful instincts are as strong as ever.

Even in our own twentieth century that boasts of its enlightenment and progress, civilized man has often reverted to the most uncivilized behavior. We have seen the sophisticated man of science, replete with all his technological gadgetry, succumb to the most barbaric forms of behavior, with education and culture powerless to hold him back. We have seen leaders of society—many of them considered custodians of morality—succumb to the most lecherous activities. It has been well said that education cannot make a devil into a saint, but it can make a devil into a clever devil! No wonder Solomon pleads with us to seek God and His wisdom, for He alone can give victory in these things.

Solomon next proceeds to give us a graphic and detailed portrait of the sensuous woman, and his strokes are bold. She is the woman who ignites the fire of lust, and then keeps fanning its flames into a conflagration. Her smooth, soothing words and the suggestive movements of her body add fuel to it. Her lips are sensuous; her body, inviting; her caresses, passionate. She is most adaptable and subtle in her ways to ingratiate her client. "Her ways are moveable, that thou canst not know them" (Proverbs 5:6). She is adept at employing the weapons of her arsenal: her words, looks, and touch. And she knows that there is one thing she *must* ensure: she must keep her client occupied. He must have no time to *think.* If he begins to think, she knows that she may well lose him. All her guile and carnal cunning is channeled in this one direction—to keep him from thinking, "lest thou shouldest ponder the path of life" (Proverbs 5:6).

"The intrusion of one serious thought might break the spell, and open the way of escape" (Charles Bridges).

SAFEGUARDS

There is nothing more important today than that men should think. Unfortunately, this is not so easy as it sounds. Many men, living the life they do and at the pace they do, spend only a minimum of their time in thinking. Indeed, to some people, the very idea of isolating themselves just to think is an unbearable proposition. Modern man does not like his own company. Or, as someone expressed it, "Modern man is afraid to get lost in thought because it is unknown territory to him!" He has been so conditioned to living in a herd that to be alone for five minutes is a touch of purgatory. If a man is alone, he must have something to look at, something to listen to, or something to feel and handle. He is no longer capable of handling a quiet moment by himself in thought. If he goes out to enjoy an afternoon in the countryside, he has to take along the transistor radio. If he drinks a cup of coffee in a cafe, he has to play around with the jukebox. If he sits at home alone, with nothing on television to please him and no magazine to titillate him, he will telephone one friend after another, just to visit.

What a waste of the wonderful cerebral factory that God has created and installed within man. The human brain with its 13 billion cells is able to handle some 15 trillion facts! No man-made computer can ever hope to match it. It has been claimed that to duplicate the human brain with man-made instruments would require 1.5 million cubic feet of girders, protons, electrons, and wires; all the water of the Mississippi River to cool it; and all the electricity of the state of Texas for a whole year to activate it. Yet God has housed this complex computer in our small physical cranium and activated it on half a volt of electricity! What power has the Creator placed at the disposal of mortal man! As far as many are concerned, however, the power remains untapped.

It goes without saying that many of the problems that beset us today and drive people to psychiatrists and different kinds of counselors could well have been avoided with a little more use of this divinely created thought machine. What is more, many of the temptations that cripple us could well have been resisted if we had spent a little more time in advance thinking. The Lord has supplied us with a graphic lesson of this truth in the parable of the prodigal son (Luke 15).

If only the prodigal had contemplated a little the ramifications of his actions before leaving home, his story would have proceeded on a far different and happier course. By acting more on impulse than reason, and by listening more to his lustful desires than to the promptings of wisdom, the prodigal made a series of wrong decisions and paid a high price for so doing. Initially, of course, there was the flurry of excitement: the new friends, the new pleasures, and the new experiences. But familiarity soon brought boredom. The day came when pleasures no longer excited him, and his sins became a surfeit. He saw banqueting tables give way to hogpens. The prodigal had made a contract with the devil, but had not read the fine print. He had not read it because he did not have the time to read it, nor the time to even think about it. At the root of the prodigal's wrong decisions was this lack of thought. He had never thought the matter through, had never thought about the effect of his actions on his father and mother—how they would grieve at his absence and worry about his safety. He never thought about the effect on his elder brother— how he would have to take on double responsibility on the farm. He never thought about the effect on his own life—how it would bring him abject poverty and starvation. As thousands have said after him: "I didn't even *think* about it."

Fortunately for the prodigal, he finally came around to doing the thing he should have done at the beginning—he began to think: "he came to himself" (Luke 15:17). The boredom of dissipation, the surfeit of sin, and the pangs of poverty all combined to force him to think. He thought of God, thought of his father, and thought of his own sinful behavior. Soon his thoughts were being translated into action, and home came the prodigal. In the words of an old Scottish preacher, the sequence was: "Sick-of-home . . . Homesick . . . Home!"

Let this also be said to the prodigal's credit: when he did begin to think, his thinking was profound enough to recognize his sin for what it really was— not just social maladjustment or moral misbehavior. His sin was basically theological. God had been the first victim of his actions. "I have sinned against heaven" (Luke 15:18). The prodigal's thinking was along the right lines, and because of this it led to sorrow and repentance. Then he proceeded from the theological to the social; the thinking that brought him back to God brought him back to his father and family. He had sinned not only against heaven, but also against his fellowmen on earth. "I have sinned against heaven, and before thee" (Luke 15:18).

One should never underestimate the power of thought. Correct thought leads to correct action, incorrect thought to incorrect action. This is the logic of Solomon: "Can a man take fire in his bosom, and his clothes not be burned?" (Proverbs 6:27). The advice of Paul a thousand years later was: "Finally, brethren, whatsoever things are true, whatsoever things are honest, whatsoever things are just, whatsoever things are pure, whatsoever things are lovely, whatsoever things are of good report; if there be any virtue, and if there be any praise, *think* on these things" (Philippians 4:8, emphasis added).

Men should not only think, but think ahead. It is inevitable that foresight is not as common nor as easy as hindsight, but it pays exceedingly high rates of return. The young man whom Solomon is addressing is reminded of the miseries that result from a life given to lust and self-gratification. If only one considered them beforehand. Think of the loss of *character:* "lest thou give thine honour unto others" (Proverbs 5:9); the loss of *time:* "and thy years unto the cruel" (Proverbs 5:9); the loss of *wealth:* "lest strangers be filled with thy wealth" (Proverbs 5:10), "for by means of a whorish woman a man is brought to a piece of bread" (Proverbs 6:26); then the loss of *freedom:* "and thy labours be in the house of a stranger" (Proverbs 5:10); and finally, the loss of one's *health:* "and thou mourn at the last, when thy flesh and thy body are consumed" (Proverbs 5:11).

Solomon makes no apology for the equation that sin means sickness. The *British Medical Journal* admitted as much some years ago when it said, "There is no tissue in the human body wholly removed from the influence of the spirit." A conclusion reached in the Bible a few thousand years earlier! Paul reminded the church at Corinth that many of their number were sick, and some were even in the cemetery years before their time for this one reason—they had sinned. Disease is often what the word says it is: *dis-ease*. Sin makes a man guilty in the eyes of God, and thus he becomes ill-at-ease in the presence of God. Think ahead, says Solomon, and mark well the price to be paid for your sins in terms of health. In addition to this, there is the question of your character, your time, your wealth, and your freedom. Loss in all these areas of life is the price you pay when you do not think ahead.

To help one overcome this craving for sexual gratification, Solomon included a further argument. As you think ahead about the anguish and misery that will result from your sin, think also of the good things you will be deprived of. Things you now enjoy and take for granted will no longer be yours. Think, for instance, of your own wife and the joy she brings to you: "And rejoice with the wife of thy youth. Let her be as the loving hind and pleasant roe . . . and be thou ravished always with her love" (Proverbs 5:18-19). Domestic love, says Solomon, is the best safeguard against the enticements of lust, but this love will be jeopardized when you visit "the strange woman." You jeopardize your home, your wife, and your children. A lifelong relationship of love is exchanged for a moment of lust.

Men should not only think and think ahead, but think still further ahead. Do not think merely of your losses for the next few years, considerable though they may be, but think of your loss for eternity. Your spiritual loss is not limited to this world; it also includes the world to come. "For the ways of man are before the eyes of the LORD, and he pondereth all his goings" (Proverbs 5:21).

In case a man should be tempted to think that he has gotten away with his sin as far as the eyes of men are concerned, Solomon reminds him of "the eyes of the LORD." The eyes of the Lord go to and fro upon the earth and see all that happens. "Neither is there any creature that is not manifest in his sight: but all things are naked and opened unto the eyes of him with whom we have to do" (Hebrews 4:13). "For God shall bring every work into judgment, with every secret thing, whether it be good, or whether it be evil" (Ecclesiastes 12:14).

The psalmist Asaph of Israel at one time was disillusioned with his situation. He had endeavored to live a righteous life, but it did not seem to bring him any of the desired results. He became a failure financially, and in his personal life as well. Other men would speak of their blessings, and how they came new every morning, but his experience was in the other direction. He was chastened every morning. The ungodly were prospering, whereas he was considered a failure. Try as he would, he could not achieve success.

Many men would have deduced from all this that godliness was no longer a paying proposition, and honesty was no longer the best policy. But rather than jump for the obvious, the psalmist returned to the sanctuary to wait upon God, and to do a little more thinking. This time his thinking paid off. God gave him the vision he needed. The psalmist not only saw ahead, but he saw further ahead than he had ever seen before; indeed, he saw to the very end of the road. He saw the destiny of the ungodly: "Then understood I *their end*" (Psalm 73:17, emphasis added).

In a similar way Solomon advises us not only to consider the temporal consequences of our immoral acts, but to look ahead and see the eternal consequences. He would have us know that our sin has been witnessed by God Himself, and that the same God will deal with it in the coming day.

Men often boast that they have gotten away with their sins, and as far as the eyes of man are concerned, they are sometimes right. But they forget the all-important factor that Solomon is here underscoring, namely, "the eyes of the LORD." When the Lord is brought into the picture, then man has never, in any sense, gotten away with his sins. Not even with *one* of his sins. If it could be proved that some person, somewhere, sometime, somehow, had gotten away with one sin—just one—it would destroy the very foundation of our faith. It would mean that every preacher might as well stop preaching, and that every church might as well close its doors. It would mean that the Bible is no longer valid, and that God Himself is no longer truthful. If a man could get away with just one sin, all would be lost. The moral foundation of the universe would collapse, and God might as well not exist. Such, of course, is not the case. Man can never get away with his sins; not with *one* of his sins; not even with the *least* of his sins. Every sin has been seen and recorded by the "eyes of the LORD."

For extra measure, Solomon added another argument that puts the punishment of sin beyond all possible doubt. Not only will God punish the sinner, but the sin will bring its own retribution as well. "His own iniquities shall take the wicked himself, and he shall be holden with the cords of his sins" (Proverbs 5:22).

Even the unbeliever, who argues that he does not believe in God and is not accountable to any divine being, is unable to dismiss the fact that sin brings its own retribution. And, of course, the fact that the unbeliever does not believe in God does not mean that God goes out of existence. Whatever he may think, God is still there, and will remain there, witnessing every act he commits. Try as he will, man can never escape from "the eyes of the LORD." Even if he could, he is still faced with the indisputable fact that his sin brings its own retribution. That he cannot deny.

What sort of retribution does sin bring with itself? We will let Solomon answer: "He shall be holden with the cords of his sins." God, according to Solomon, does not need a prison to hold the sinner, chains to bind him, or fetters to shackle him; a man's own sins do it for Him. His own sins tie the cords around the sinner. At first, the process is hardly perceptible; indeed, it may go unnoticed. But as each sin is committed, the cord is tightened a little more firmly and the knot is made a little more secure. It is only a matter of time before the sinner becomes a prisoner of his own sin. What he started out doing as a voluntary act, he now does as an involuntary habit. Step by step, the volunteer has become a conscript.

It has been said that there are only two stages in the life of an alcoholic: (a) when he could stop if he would; (b) when he would stop if he could. That is exactly what Solomon says. The more often we sin, the tighter the cords. Then the moment inevitably arrives when our freedom to act and our will to resist have disappeared forever. We may still strive and struggle for a while, but it is to no avail: "he is holden with the cords of his sin."

Milton touched upon the same truth in his immortal epic *Paradise Lost* (1, 212-20). Not only sinful man, but Satan himself discovers the truth that evil turns ultimately upon its progenitor.

> And high permission of all-ruling Heaven
> Left him at large to his own dark designs,
> That with reiterated crimes he might
> Heap on himself damnation, while he sought
> Evil to others, and enrag'd might see
> How all his malice serv'd but to bring forth
> Infinite goodness, grace and mercy shown
> On Man by him seduc't, but on himself
> Treble confusion, wrath and vengeance pour'd.

But surely man cannot be abandoned in such a state. He cannot be left bound in the cords of his sin without any hope of deliverance. If the gospel is good news, then it must have something good to say even to these prisoners. When the cords get tighter and tighter, and escape becomes an impossibility, surely there must be something that can be done. As long as the prisoner breathes, is there no hope?

Thank God there is. As long as the prisoner breathes there is hope: hope that he can still think, and continue to think, and carry on thinking, until he finally reaches the point at which his thinking becomes a petition to God. When he reaches that stage and is able to say with the prodigal "I have sinned," then there is hope—sure hope. The God who has mercy to offer the repentant sinner is also the God who is able to break the sinner's cords and snap asunder his fetters. The forgiving Savior is also the Lion of Judah who can

> . . . break ev'ry chain,
> And give to us the victory again and again.

Proverbs 20:1
Wine is a mocker, strong drink is raging:
and whosoever is deceived thereby is not wise.

4

SOCIAL DRINKING?

Why Solomon tarried so long before mentioning one of the greatest of all social vices, drunkenness, has always intrigued commentators. Not until chapter 20 is this particular sin mentioned in the book of Proverbs. Other vices have already been exposed and underscored many times over. It is only now that he faces the question of strong drink.

Some believe Solomon waited to discuss alcohol because drunkenness was not a major problem in his day, and thus was well down on his list of priorities. That, however, is a difficult proposition to accept. We know that this sin appeared very early in biblical history: Noah was guilty of it, and so was Lot. It would be truly amazing if it was not prevalent in Solomon's day, especially since it was a time of prosperity in Israel. He did, however, finally come to this sin in chapter 20, and he returned to it in chapter 23. King Lemuel also discussed it in Proverbs 31.

ABSTINENCE VERSUS MODERATION

All Christians today—whether liberal or conservative, progressive or traditional—recognize the evil of drunkenness. Drunkenness, like every other excess, is a sin. Period. The division comes not on the question of drunkenness, but on the question of total ab-

stinence. Should one abstain completely from all
strong drink, or can one drink socially and imbibe
moderately without the risk of ruining one's testimony? That is the dividing issue: *abstinence* or
moderation?

Both sides can produce data, and both sides can
quote Scripture. There is plenty of Scripture to quote.
As a matter of fact, half of the books of the Bible refer
to this subject. It is given greater attention in the Bible
than the sins of pride, cheating, stealing, adultery, or
blasphemy.

The advocates of moderation will invariably cite
the instances of Jesus turning water into wine at Cana
of Galilee and using wine at the institution of the Last
Supper. All would agree that the wine used was not
unfermented grape juice. (Grape juice without refrig-
eration automatically turns into wine.) The same
people will quote Matthew 11:18-19, in which account the citizens of Israel drew a contrast between
John the Baptist and Jesus. John the Baptist was a
Nazarite, abstaining completely from all strong drink;
but of Jesus they said: "Behold a man gluttonous, and
a winebibber, a friend of publicans and sinners." They
will also quote 1 Timothy 5:23, in which Paul advises
Timothy to "drink no longer water, but use a little
wine for thy stomach's sake and thine often infir-
mities."

Advocates of moderation will allow that total abstinence was the norm for certain dedicated souls who
had taken the Nazarite vow, but it certainly was not
the standard for all people. Furthermore, they will
claim that if church membership demands total abstinence, then many of our Reformed and Puritan
forefathers would have to be thrown out of the church.
So would our Lord Himself!

Those who plead for total abstinence, on the other hand, will admit that "wine" in the New Testament was not unfermented grape juice, but they will at the same time insist that it was a far different kind of wine from that in use today. In Bible days, wine was invariably mixed with water, the ratio being anything from two to five parts water to one part wine. Only barbarians drank wine unmixed. This may be the reason the Old Testament distinguishes between "wine" and "strong drink" (Leviticus 10:8-9; Numbers 6:3). Wine was always diluted. The Talmud states that the wine that every Jew drank during the Passover feast was to be mixed in the ratio of three parts water to one part wine. It would be a fair assumption that the same mixture was used at the institution of the Lord's Supper.

There is an interesting comment in 2 Maccabees 15:39, in which nonbiblical account it is said: "It is harmful to drink wine alone, or again, to drink water alone." In ancient times, as indeed in many lands today, it was not always safe to drink water by itself. The safest and easiest method to make it safe for drinking was to mix it with wine. Wine acted as a purifying agent. One of the early church Fathers, Justin Martyr (c. A.D. 150), described the Lord's Supper in this way: "Bread is brought, and wine and water." And Cyprian (c. A.D. 250) said: "Thus, therefore, in considering the cup of the Lord, water alone cannot be offered, even as wine alone cannot be offered. For if anyone offers wine only, the blood of Christ is dissociated from us: but if the water be alone, the people are dissociated from Christ . . . thus the cup of the Lord is not indeed water alone, nor wine alone, unless each be mingled with the other."

You may well ask, What is the whole point of this argument? It is this: there is a vast difference between the potency of alcoholic beverages today and the potency of wine in New Testament days. One would have to drink over twenty-two glasses of that wine (mixed with three parts water) to equal the alcoholic content of two martinis today. Or, as William Arnot said over a hundred years ago, "To quote from the English Bible a text about ancient Judean wine in support of modern Scottish whiskey, is not right, and cannot long be successful."

In addition to the above, the advocates of total abstinence can produce a list of staggering statistics that proves the evil results of alcoholism. They point to statistics showing there are 9.5 million alcoholics in America who fill up our hospitals, mental institutions, and penitentiaries. To be an alcoholic is to be, more often than not, a man who has lost his job, his family, his friends, and his health. If he has not reached skid row, he is going in that direction. Half of the traffic deaths on the highways are drink-related. According to the American Medical Association, "One ounce of alcohol in the body increases the chances of having an automobile accident by more than 1,000 percent." One-third of our air accidents, one-half of our homicides, and three-quarters of our home breakups are drink-related.

There is not the least doubt that drink spawns crime. Many if not most of the criminals incarcerated in our prisons are there for this one reason. It has been demonstrated time and again that no business in the world can compete with the brewing industry for producing criminals. Bear in mind that there are over one hundred thousand more alcoholic beverage outlets in the United States than the combined total of churches, synagogues, and temples.

Combine all these statistics and a man may well ask: Can any good thing be said for alcohol?

Some assert that there is a dual tradition in Scripture: one that counsels moderation and allows so-called social drinking, and one that counsels total abstinence. If that is the case, it makes it difficult for the individual believer to know which way to act. If there are two counsels, and both are valid, what is a man to do? Or do the two counsels ultimately emerge as one? Or could it be that one counsel carries more evidence than the other?

These questions can best be answered by investigating the kinds of guidance that are given in Scripture. It will then be clear that ultimately there is no duality and no contradiction, but merely two sides to the one coin.

The believer finds that there are at least three things to guide him as he searches the Scriptures: biblical practices, biblical precepts, and biblical principles. We have already seen that biblical practices and biblical precepts have been quoted by advocates of both positions. We are thus left with biblical *principles.* What do they say? Obviously, they have to be the deciding factor in the case.

Lest anyone should imagine that this approach is artificial, it should be borne in mind that the same procedure has been used concerning other problems as well. One example would be that of slavery. Biblical practices and biblical precepts were quoted on both sides of the issue of slavery; ultimately, it was biblical principles that decided the issue for the Christian world. Men came to realize that the underlying principles of the Word of God were against, rather than for, slavery.

What, then, is the biblical principle concerning strong drink? Bearing in mind the difference in potency between wine in the Bible and modern day alcoholic beverages; bearing in mind the teaching of the

Bible on the question of the "weaker brother"; bearing in mind also that the Bible considers drunkenness not merely a disease but a sin; it is then not difficult to conclude that biblical principles are on the side of total abstinence.

THE GREAT DECEIT

Accepting this premise, we find corroboration in the wisdom of Solomon when he says, "Wine is a mocker" (Proverbs 20:1). Strong drink, in the opinion of this man, is deceitful to the ultimate degree. It will impoverish a man; impair his judgment; compound his problems; and betray his secrets. In the words of Thomas Fuller, it "turns a man inside outwards."

All the claims made on behalf of strong drink are riddled with deceit. This is why Solomon underscores the fact in a dogmatic, categorical statement: "Wine is a mocker." It deceives.

One might ask at this point, In what way does it deceive us, since we are all conversant with its results? The facts are all too evident. But that is exactly what does happen: facts or no facts, men are still deceived by the claims made in the name of alcohol.

William Arnot, in his book *Laws from Heaven for Life on Earth,* referred to five ways in which men are deceived by the claims of strong drink.

Deceit number one. It is claimed that alcohol is nourishing. But strong drink is nothing of the sort. As a matter of fact, it is the very opposite of nourishing—it helps to destroy man's food potential. The grain and fruit that are cultivated for the production of alcohol mean there is so much less land to grow food upon. The harmfulness of this situation is never more evident than in our present day, when countless millions of people face the grim prospect of starvation. It is claimed that starvation already takes its toll at the rate of ten thousand people per day, and predictions are that the situation will be aggravated by many millions more in the years ahead. God commanded the earth to bring forth and supply the needs of man, but due to man's greed for drink, much land has been misappropriated to provide fodder for breweries and distilleries. If this is not a major deceit, what is?

Deceit number two. It is said that alcohol has a medicinal value. There may be some element of truth in this, within given limits, as Paul's advice to Timothy that he should take a little wine for his stomach's sake attests. But the claim that strong drink has a highly curative quality is certainly exaggerated. Science has no doubt on the matter: rather than add to our physical strength and sustenance, alcohol subtracts from it. Although it may give a man a feeling of well-being and ignite his courage, it is all transitory, and ultimately it will deprive the body, not build it. Alcohol never adds to a man's strength, and certainly not to his days. As a matter of fact, the opposite is the case: it saps his strength and shortens his days.

Alcohol is now considered the number three killer in the nation, outranked only by heart disease and cancer. General Pershing claimed that "Drunkenness has killed more men than all of history's wars." And all the time it claims to be of curative value! No wonder Shakespeare called it a poison that "men take into the mouth to steal away the brain." He was restating what Solomon had said three thousand years earlier: "Wine is a mocker." It makes extravagant claims, but all are proved false by the ensuing results.

Deceit number three. Alcohol is said to be a great source of revenue. Americans spend three million dollars per hour on alcoholic beverages—more on booze than on bread. According to a prediction by the

Roper Company (which conducted a study at the request of the American Distilling Company), by the year 2000 there will be bars in churches, beauty salons, hospitals, public transportation stations, department stores, parks, and colleges. By then the "stars and stripes" may well be renamed the "stars and bars"!

The argument is frequently heard: "Consider the revenue brought into the treasury by the tax imposed on alcoholic beverages." It sounds impressive: $8 billion per year. The third largest source of tax revenue in the nation. But pause a moment: there is another side to the ledger. Eight billion dollars come in from alcohol, but $25 billion go out to pay for the results of alcoholism. This is measured in terms of absenteeism from work, low industrial production, automobile accidents, medical care of victims, welfare support for destitute orphans, penitentiary upkeep for liquor-incited criminals, institutions for lunatics, and so on—and that does not include the trauma of broken homes and maimed lives. What sort of a business is it that drains three times as much money out of the treasury as it puts in? And who makes up the deficiency? The taxpayer does, of course. As B. Charles Hostetter once said, "There is something irrational in our system when the state licenses a saloon keeper to make drunken paupers, and then taxes sober men to take care of them." Follow the argument further: it is even more irrational for the state to license someone to sell that which will make a man drunk, and then punish the man for being drunk. It was Solomon who said it, and we corroborate it: "Wine is a mocker."

Deceit number four. Alcohol producers claim their product is a stimulant of cheer and camaraderie. At first it does seem to cause a geniality in which conversation is easy and a festive spirit prevails, but ultimately no true fellowship can be based on such an artificial stimulant. Continue the stimulant for a little while and see what happens: the camaraderie degenerates into quarrels; the bonhomie into brawls; the fellowship into feuds. Before the end, the cup of fun becomes the cup of fury. Men will act like beasts: Lot became incestuous, Ahasuerus ribald, and Herod a murderer. It is far better *to be* a beast than to *act like* a beast. It has been well said that the veneer of civilization is so thin that a little alcohol will rub it off.

Deceit number five. It is said that alcohol is a mark of social prestige and status. This, of all the claims, is the most deceitful. To overthrow the argument, all one needs to do is take a five-minute stroll on skid row; if not skid row, then a state prison; or, if not one of these, then one of the hundreds of insane asylums scattered throughout our land. If drinking is a mark of social distinction, then the saying is true: "A Bowery bum is just someone who tried too hard to be a man of distinction." Ask any of the people in one of the above-mentioned places if drink leads to prestige and position, and they will reply with a deafening unanimity: "It is a lie. Drink leads to shame, disgrace, poverty, and prison." They could well add: "a lost eternity."

Upton Sinclair, in his book *The Cup of Fury,* said: "It has been my fate to live among drinking people: novelists, poets, playwrights and stars of stage and screen. I have seen two-score of them go to their doom. . . . I put before the public this tragic record of a half-century of genius, twisted and tortured by alcohol. I ask that it be read with one fact always in the back of the reader's mind: the fact that three out of four of the students in college today are drinkers."[1] Sinclair then proceeded to name names: Jack London, Sinclair Lewis, O. Henry, John Barrymore, Douglas

Fairbanks, Eugene O'Neill, Dylan Thomas, and others.

There is one ingredient in this whole problem that is a mark of our generation. Thanks to television and radio, the beer baron now has direct access to our houses. He makes maximum use of the opportunity. Besides this, his products are purchasable in every corner store and supermarket. His promotional gimmickery sounds so exciting, progressive, and prestigious, but he never tells you that his product has the power to enslave you, physically and spiritually. What is more, his product does not give up until the victim is disgraced and degraded. And even that is not the end. The Bible tells us that ultimately the drunkard is damned. When he arrives at his final destination, he finds himself cast out of God's presence forever, with none of his former companions able to help him. Make no mistake: no drunkard will enter heaven (1 Corinthians 6:9-10). With such a record, it is any wonder that President Abraham Lincoln said that "liquor may have many defenders, but no defense."

Yet in spite of all the negative evidence, the average man will continue with his strong drink as he always has done, and all for one, simple reason: *he likes it*. What drink does to his palate is more important to him than what it does to his family, his business, his health—even his destiny. Arguments carry little hope against appetite.

THE ROAD TO RECOVERY

In view of such deceit and such a record, does the Bible offer any hope to the dupes of drink? Does it have a word for the alcoholic? Does the God who hates the sin but loves the sinner have counsel to give on the problem?

God always has counsel to give. For one thing, God knows that man is incapable of conquering the desire for alcohol on his own; he needs direct, divine help. That is why we are counseled in Scripture, "And be not drunk with wine, wherein is excess; but be filled with the Spirit" (Ephesians 5:18). When that happens, we find that greater is He that is in us, than any power outside that tries to destroy us.

For another thing, God counsels us to have no fellowship with drunkards. "Be not among winebibbers" (Proverbs 23:20). Some people will react to this and say, "But surely we must be friendly toward all people, even to publicans and sinners. Isn't that the example Jesus left us?" Yes it is, but with this proviso: no friendship should involve compromise of principle or participation in questionable habits. Christ came to save people *from* their sins, not to condone them *in* their sins (Romans 13:13).

Finally, God counsels us to keep on remembering the end results. Just as Solomon said in Proverbs: "Look not thou upon the wine when it is red, when it giveth his colour in the cup, when it moveth itself aright. At the last it biteth like a serpent, and stingeth like an adder" (Proverbs 23:31-32). Alcohol promises great things, but its real character is not revealed until it is too late. *"At the last* it biteth" (emphasis added). If the serpent did bite right away, who would venture near her? The serpent is known for her cunning; it is at the last that she bites.

It is time to tell it like it is. If the last results of alcoholism—the broken homes; maimed lives; orphaned children; dregs of skid row; cells on death row; yes, and the mocking devils of hell—were put on display at the beginning, I predict that every customer would flee the bar, and every beer baron be bankrupt overnight. Such things, of course, are not likely to happen for the simple reason that "Wine is a mocker."

Proverbs 11:24
There is that scattereth,
and yet increaseth;
and there is that withholdeth more than is meet,
but it tendeth to poverty.

5

IS TITHING A GOOD INVESTMENT?

A story that was given much mileage in the media was that of a certain Hugh McNatt of Miami, Florida. He heard the pastor of his church promise the congregation that "blessings, benefits, and rewards would come to a person who tithed 10 percent of his wealth." Being a pragmatist, Hugh McNatt did exactly what the preacher suggested. He withdrew $800 of his savings and gave it to the church. He then sat back and waited for the dividends to come in. They never did come in, however, and Hugh McNatt became disillusioned. He sued the church in county court.

Two questions have to be asked here: (a) Does the New Testament teach that tithing Christians will invariably be financially recompensed? (b) Is a preacher justified in offering material inducements in order to increase his church finances? The answer to both these questions has to be negative. Nowhere does the Bible teach that the believer who lives the life of faith and gives of his earnings to Christ and His church will invariably be blessed with *material* riches. And nowhere is a preacher commissioned to dangle the bait of material inducements to entice souls into the spiritual Kingdom of Christ.

The error of Hugh McNatt was the error of the psalmist Asaph of Israel on one occasion. In Psalm 73 he complained to God: "I was envious at the foolish, when I saw the prosperity of the wicked. . . . Behold, these are the ungodly, who prosper in the world; they increase in riches. Verily I have cleansed my heart in vain, and washed my hands in innocency" (Psalm 73:3, 12-13). The psalmist could not understand why the ungodly should have been prospering in that manner when he, who had lived a godly life, had been denied those blessings. But rather than sue the Temple, the psalmist returned to the Temple to pray. It was then that he realized that the reward of the righteous is not to be measured by material wealth but rather by the fellowship and favor of God.

In case someone should deduce from this that the life of faith always leads to poverty, however, let it be added immediately that the life of faith is far more likely to lead to prosperity. As a matter of fact, it is the life of sin, selfishness, and greed that is likely to lead to poverty. The man who obeys God is the man who will be blessed of God. The man who gives is the man who gets. This is what Solomon is saying here in Proverbs 11:24: "There is that scattereth, and yet increaseth; and there is that withholdeth more than is meet, but it tendeth to poverty."

All men know that liberality is a good way of winning friends, but Solomon named another advantage: liberality is a good way of winning financial returns as well. In the words of Charles Bridges, "Bounty is the way to plenty."

It is never easy, of course, for a hardheaded businessman to accept a proposition like this—that material wealth is governed by spiritual laws. After all, who could possibly operate his business on this "irrational" dictum of Solomon? It is like saying, "Give away and make a profit." That seems to be a guaranteed shortcut to the bankruptcy court. Yet there is no denying that however irrational it may seem, it is the law of God, and what is more, a law that still operates. The Bible makes it abundantly clear that a man must give if he is to get. He must divide his possessions if he is to multiply them.

> A man there was, and they called him mad;
> The more he gave, the more he had.
>
> JOHN BUNYAN

Paul Larsen has supplied a most apt illustration of this truth in his book,[1] in which he told of his brother who was a pastor of a church in southern California. One night an arsonist set fire to the church and burned the whole edifice to the ground, including all the pastor's books and sermon notes that he had been accumulating over the years. Now books can be replaced, but sermon notes? It so happened, however, that this brother was an addictive mimeographer who had made copies of all his sermons for the benefit of others. Because of that generosity, Larsen and a dozen other people had complete files of those sermons. After the fire, Larsen went to visit his brother and presented to him all the sermon notes that he had received. His brother was completely overwhelmed, and when able to speak he stuttered, "You know, the only thing I have of my past is what I gave to other people."

Just as the old saying goes, the only things we ever keep are the things we give away.

Martin Luther said something similar in the sixteenth century when he remarked, "I have held many things in my hands and have lost them all; but whatever I have in God's hands, that I still possess." It was this very truth that Solomon conveyed to his readers three thousand years ago: "There is that scattereth, and yet increaseth; and there is that withholdeth more than is meet, but it tendeth to poverty" (Proverbs 11:24). The same truth was corroborated by Paul when he told the Corinthians: "He which soweth sparingly shall reap also sparingly; and he which soweth boun- tifully shall reap also bountifully" (2 Corinthians 9:6). And, of course, it was the Lord of all who said: "Give, and it shall be given unto you; good measure, pressed down, and shaken together, and running over, shall men give into your bosom" (Luke 6:38). He not only said it, but He also practiced it.

Jesus and Alexander died at thirty-three!
The Greek made all men slaves; the Jew made all men free!
One built a throne on blood; the other built on love.
The one was born of earth; the other from above.
One conquered all the earth, to lose all earth and heaven;
The other gave up all, that all to Him be given.
The Greek forever died; the Jew forever lives!
He loses all who gets, and wins all things who gives!
AUTHOR UNKNOWN

Every law, of course, can be misconstrued and misused, and this law is no exception. It is quite pos- sible to find a man who will say, "Since this law promises to be a foolproof way of making money, I'll try it. I'll contribute to the church, not from any great love for the church, but because it is a subtle way to get rich. I'll do exactly as they say: I'll give in order to get." Shades of Hugh McNatt! But proceed no further. The man who is out to prostitute the principles of God will never succeed; he will not get rich materially nor be blessed spiritually. God is fully aware of his cun- ning plans and disreputable motives and will not be outmaneuvered by any such puny schemes. Make no mistake, the man who tries to manipulate God and pervert His laws will never get rich, and he may well lose his original deposit in the bargain. Benevolence must never be used as a merchandise, nor liberality as a lever. Joseph Parker was right when he warned us not to "yoke generosity to the chariot of Mammon."

One cannot help but believe that God had foreseen such a misuse of His law. That could be the reason He did not couch this law in more rigid and inflexible terms. As a matter of fact, this law is so expressed that it allows a good deal of leeway. It is just as if God were saying: "This is not a cast-iron, foolproof formula that works for everyone, everywhere, and under every possible condition. Rather, it is a general principle, flexible and adaptable, that allows many exceptions." Note how Solomon expressed it: "There is that scattereth, and yet increaseth; and there is that withholdeth more than is meet, but it tendeth to poverty." He does not say that withholding will invariably lead to poverty. What he does say is that it *tendeth* to poverty.

This law of God must obviously be understood in a general and ideal sense. It offers no foolproof warranty that Christian generosity will invariably lead to increased riches. If such were the case, it would just be an insurance policy, and faith could be dismissed as a vestige. What Solomon is saying is that it is a general, divine principle that a generous man will reap generously, and a tightfisted man will reap sparingly.

This law can be demonstrated in many areas. It is seen, for example, in the world of nature. The farmer is conversant with it as he plans for harvest. He knows that he has to put seed into the ground if he is to get a harvest from the ground. He knows also that he has to supply the land with the necessary fertilizer, or his crops will be meager. The farmer knows better than anyone that the more liberal and generous his outlay, the better his crops and the fuller his barns. The more he scattereth, the more he increaseth. He knows that he has to give if he is to get.

This law that applies to nature is equally germane to human nature. It is the key that unlocks those God-given secrets that so often elude us.

KEY TO HAPPINESS

Giving is the key to happiness. Although we often refer to the pursuit of happiness, experience soon teaches us that such a pursuit is worse than futile. Happiness may be pursued, but never, never is it caught. Countless people have tried the experiment, and have gone in pursuit of happiness with bated breath, only to find that it eluded them. Try as they would, they were never able to overtake it. It foiled their every attempt. Those people fell victim to the illusion that happiness comes by getting. But happiness does not come that way. Happiness comes by giving. It is when people decide to give happiness to others that they unexpectedly realize it for themselves.

Man, for whatever reason, does not seem to have the capacity to make himself happy, or else every man would be happy. However, if he is unable to make himself happy, he does have the capacity to make other people happy. That he can do. When he does that, he unwittingly discovers the grand secret: by making others happy, he finds happiness for himself.

This is the kind of happiness that will persist independently of all outward circumstances, and even in spite of all outward circumstances. The so-called happiness that the world talks about depends so much on a man's condition and circumstances. Let him lose his job, his position, his wealth, or his health, and he has lost his happiness. His happiness is dependent on his circumstances. This is not so with the happiness that God gives His people. God-given happiness survives irrespective of conditions or circumstances. It survives unemployment, poverty, pain, and suffering. Indeed, it not only survives, it thrives. This is why we read of saints who were able to rejoice in tribulation, become buoyant in adversity, and sing praises in prisons.

F. R. Malty once said that Jesus promised His disciples three things; namely, that they would be: (a) completely fearless; (b) in constant trouble; and (c) absurdly happy. There it is: constant trouble—absurdly happy. It is a happiness that continues irrespective of all outward and untoward circumstances. The key to obtaining such happiness? One gives to get.

There is an old spiritual that goes: "Nobody knows the trouble I've seen." Fortunately, it does not end there, or it would be just another melancholy dirge, devoid of all hope for the future. The author added two more words to his line, and by so doing immortalized his song. Those two words bring the vision of victory to the valley of defeat. In the opinion of Walter Hampden, the addition of those two words has made it the most memorable sentence in the English language. "Nobody knows the trouble I've seen—" and who can deny it? When the Black man goes in search of his roots, he finds the slave owner and the plantation, the slave-ship captain and the irons, the slave trader and the whips. Stolen from his wife and little children and shipped away to an alien land, never to set eyes on them again, the Black slave gave vent to his heartbreak in these spirituals. "Nobody knows the trouble I've seen." But the genius of that line is in the two words that follow—genius, and more than genius. Here you find the heartbeat of the Christian faith. "Nobody knows the trouble I've seen, *Glory,*

Hallelujah.'' That is it. Having found God, the slave had found a happiness that was independent of all his pain and misery. He had constant trouble all right, but he could be absurdly happy.

In the same spirit Paul told the Philippians, "For I have learned, in whatsoever state I am, therewith to be content" (Philippians 4:11). If you can improve your circumstances, by all means do so; but if you cannot change them, learn to accept them as part of the program of God for your life.

Listen to old Habakkuk the prophet in the day when bankruptcy stared him in the face: "Although the fig tree shall not blossom, neither shall fruit be in the vines; the labour of the olive shall fail, and the fields shall yield no meat; the flock shall be cut off from the fold, and there shall be no herd in the stalls: yet I will rejoice in the LORD, I will joy in the God of my salvation" (Habakkuk 3:17-18).

Nothing can keep the saints under. Give them poverty and even penury, pain and punishment, shackles and fetters—yes, even prisons and gallows—and they come back singing "Glory, Hallelujah."

KEY TO MATURITY

Giving is the key to maturity. It is a baby who wants, demands, and insists. An infallible sign of babyhood is engaging in tantrums until one gets what one wants. The mature person acts very differently. He does not scream for his rights or holler for attention—he has managed to outgrow such childish behavior. The mature man has learned the secret that one never gets by getting: one gets by giving.

Have you ever stopped to consider why God asked His people for a tithe of their earnings? Obviously, He does not need it for Himself. God could well exist without our contributions. Nevertheless, He has seen fit to institute the practice of tithing, and to ask His people to lay aside that part of their income so it can be used for His purposes. But God's purposes do not mean God's benefit. God had other reasons in mind.

One reason, of course, was that the Temple ministry had to be maintained. Another reason was that the poor and needy had to be supported. But there was still another reason, as important—if not more so — as any of the others. The tithe was intended to be a means of blessing to the tither himself; as a matter of fact, the tither benefits more than anyone else from his tithe. God can well afford not to receive the tithe, but can the believer afford not to give it? Tithing is a process that contributes to the believer's spiritual maturity. So when he withholds his tithe from the Lord, the believer actually is hurting himself, not the Lord. He is denying himself something that is vital for his Christian character.

We are told in Scripture that God made the Sabbath for man, and not man for the Sabbath. So with tithing. It was made for man's own benefit, that he might grow and mature in the things of the Spirit. There is a negative blessing also: tithing insulates a man from the evils of covetousness. Being taught and encouraged to give helps him to overcome the temptation of avarice.

This is why the giving of tithes and offerings has been an integral part of man's worship from the very beginning. Actually, there can be no worship without it, for worship is essentially giving. One gives oneself, one's time, and one's money. As for our time, God asks for one part in seven; as for our possessions, one part in ten. By giving of these things, one gives of himself. A man's time and treasure represent parts of the man himself.

This then is what pleases the Lord concerning the practice of tithing: not so much the tithe itself, but the tither. It is in the act of giving that a man reveals the dimensions of his love for God. It is here that his character is on display. Read a man's check stubs and you find what really counts in his life; money not only talks, but it talks about him!

Let's look at an example. Imagine a man who finds himself with $1,000 to spare. What is he going to do with it: spend it, invest it, or give it away? Whatever he does, he is going to reveal his character by the action he takes. If he decides to spend it on himself or his family, no one will blame him. It is his to spend. If he decides to invest it, he is still blameless. It is his to invest. There may be a rainy day coming, and he wants to be prepared. But suppose he does not spend or invest it, and instead decides to give it away. That act in itself will tell you a great deal about the character of the man. It will tell you that whatever else he may be, he is certainly not greedy or selfish but a man with a generous side to his nature. Suppose he gives the thousand dollars to further the Lord's work in the world? That will tell you even more about him. It will tell you that here is a dedicated man, a man who not only believes in God but believes that God has first claim on all his possessions. It will tell you that here is a just steward, a steward who will not be ashamed of his transactions in the coming day when the books are opened. It will tell you that here is a man mature in the Spirit, a man who has overcome the temptations of the flesh. Indeed, here is a man who has learned the grand secret of the saints, that one gives if one is to get. How true the saying: "We make a living from what we get; we make a life from what we give."

Giving is the key to blessing. God has decreed that there are two conditions for blessing, and they are enshrined for us in two New Testament verses:

1. "Ask, and it shall be given you" (Matthew 7:7).

2. "Give, and it shall be given unto you" (Luke 6:38).

Does this explain the paucity of our blessings today? Can it be that we have kept the first condition and ignored the second? Prayed but not tithed? Asked but not given? There is no doubt that many of God's people have withheld from God that which is rightfully His, and by so doing have deprived themselves of the blessing of God upon their lives.

There is an inscription over a cathedral altar in France that reads: "He that bringeth no gift to the altar, beareth no blessing away." It is our giving to God that opens the door for God to give to us. If our giving be little, God's door will be opened but a little. "And with what measure ye mete, it shall be measured to you again" (Matthew 7:2).

It cannot be emphasized too strongly that in order to get the blessing of God upon our lives, the same law applies here as with happiness and maturity: one has to give to get. This truth cannot be more clearly and specifically stated than in the Savior's own words: "Give, and it shall be given unto you." This is more than faith; this is faith in action. This is more than asking; this is giving. Words can be cheap, and even prayer at times comes too readily; it is when we give of ourselves and our possessions that the great blessings begin to flow.

This truth, of course, is no closely guarded secret; as a matter of fact, it is written large on the pages of

Holy Scripture, and written often. It has been claimed that the concept of giving is referred to in the Bible no less than 1,520 times. What is more, it is a concept that has been demonstrated in the lives of Christian men and women throughout history. In our time, R. G. LeTourneau applied this law, tithed his income to God, and saw God restore it to him a hundredfold. So did John D. Rockefeller, who from an original salary of five dollars a week advanced to become the founder of one of the greatest financial empires of all time. So did William Colgate, who left home penniless as a young man but who lived to make a fortune after fortune in the soap business. So did H. J. Heinz, who from peddling his mother's horseradish became famous for his "57 varieties" and his vast fortune. The same is true with J. L. Kraft of cheese-making fame, Henry P. Crowell of Quaker Oats fame, and hundreds of others. These men all shared the same formula: they took God as their partner and saw that the first tenth of their income went to Him. They soon discovered that this spiritual law is as operative as the physical laws that sustain us. They all believed with complete conviction that one has to give if one is to get.

Indeed, one may venture a step further and assert that not only does one have to give in order to get, but one has to give in order to live—certainly to live the kind of life God intends for us. This truth cannot be better illustrated than by a story told by that doyen of southern preachers, Dr. R. G. Lee.

Dr. Lee tells of a chronic complainer who always moaned: "Our churches cost too much; I am sick and tired of it."

"Yes," said another, "but I want to tell you a story out of my own life. Some years ago a baby boy came into my house, and from the time he was born he cost me something. I had to buy food and clothing and medicine, and after a while, toys and a puppy dog. When he started to school, he cost me more and more; and when he started to college, the costs were still greater and greater; and later he began going out with girls, and you know how much that costs! Then in his senior year he suddenly died, and since then he has not cost me a cent."

When next I feel like complaining, I am going to remind myself of that story. I am going to remind myself that it costs nothing to worship a dead God, and nothing to operate a dead church. By my tithing, I am actually doing much more than I thought I was doing. I am not only making it possible for God to bless me, but I am proclaiming to the world that my God is alive. I am also proclaiming by the same token that the church is alive and at work in the lives of men.

Proverbs 13:24
He that spareth his rod hateth his son:
but he that loveth him chasteneth him betimes.

,

6

IS IT RIGHT TO SPANK?

Let's admit it: it is much easier to spare the rod. It is much easier to say yes to your child than to endure his tantrums. In this way you ensure harmony in the home, with no bickering, arguments, or quarrels. How wonderful to have a home set on a no-collision course, a home about which the neighbors will remark: "What beautiful people!" It is much easier to spare the rod.

THE GREAT EXPERIMENT

It is no wonder that Dr. Spock's book *Baby and Child Care* achieved great popularity, exceeding the 28 million mark in sales. Dr. Spock convinced a whole generation of fathers and mothers that permissiveness was the right policy. Children were merely passing through phases and in time would outgrow their tantrums. As a result, discipline became a dirty word and corporal punishment was out. Yes, it is much easier to spare the rod.

And so the experiment has been tried. For years now Dr. Spock's principles have been put into practice, with fathers and mothers throwing away the birch, the paddle, and the cane. They sat back in comfort as their children grew up according to the new rules, or lack of rules. What has been the result of all this? Nothing but a generation of rowdy and rebellious youth, defying authority, irritating their elders, and insulting their parents.

Jerry Rubin, one of the notorious Chicago Seven, stated on the Kent State University campus, "The first part of the Yippie program, you know, is kill your parents, because until you're prepared to kill your parents, you're not really prepared to change the country, because our parents are our first oppressors." Two weeks later, May 1970, the campus erupted in violence, and four students were killed.

Did not Jesus forewarn us that one of the signs of the last days would be that of children hating their parents? We see one of the effects of it in our generation: children rebelling at home, and then carrying their rebellion from the home to the kindergarten, on to the grade school, to the high school, to the college, to the street, and finally, to the courthouse and the penitentiary. In American schools each year there are shootings, stabbings, assaults, rapes, and vandalism with total damages of more than one-half billion dollars. Children want to tear down what their parents sacrificed to build up. In some areas, armed guards have been called in to patrol school corridors.

Senator Birch Bayh recently released a preliminary subcommittee report on vandalism in American schools. The title of the report is significant in itself: "Our Nation's Schools—a Report Card: 'A' In School Violence and Vandalism." The report is a shocker, underscoring the problems of drug addiction, rape, robbery, gang violence, alcoholism, prostitution, and blackmail. As the senator himself said, it reads "like a casualty list from a war zone or a vice-squad annual report." Seventy thousand teachers are assaulted each year in our public school classrooms, and hundreds of thousands of students are assaulted. One hundred persons are murdered each year in our schools.

Over in the United Kingdom, the situation is parallel. A British government report revealed that 88 percent of London schoolboys are thieves, with total thefts averaging out to more than one hundred per schoolboy-thief. Then follows the understatement of the decade: "These kids are our future, and if we can't find a healthy outlet for them, we are in trouble."

The late J. Edgar Hoover added another element to the category of youthful lawlessness when he said, "Youth crimes have not only increased in number, but also in viciousness. Kids today are showing a total disregard for life and property."

The results have been so shocking, and the statistics so staggering, that even Dr. Spock has had a change of mind. He now tells us: "I don't like misbehaved children. I don't like children who are rude, or who are self-centered. I'm certainly not a permissivist." He then added that what has actually happened is that parents have lost the ability to be firm. "We didn't know until it was too late how our know-it-all attitude was undermining the self-assurance of parents." And again: "Submissiveness only encourages children to be more difficult and makes the parents more resentful . . . until they explode in anger!"

Results from a recent Gallup survey support Dr. Spock's words. Five and one-half million fathers and mothers went on record stating that their children are more trouble than they are worth. Of the thousands of parents who wrote to Ann Landers in answer to her question, "If you had it to do over, would you have children?" 70 percent emphatically said no. Ann Landers said that such a response was the greatest shock she had ever experienced. It is increasingly obvious that modern parents are not enjoying their children.

Neither do many of them understand their children. They would probably agree with John Wilmot, of Rochester, who said back in the seventeenth century: "Before I got married I had six theories about bringing up children; now I have six children and no theories!"

BRINGING BACK THE ROD?

With all these grim statistics that shock and dishearten us, is there not a danger now of a reaction setting in, and of parents becoming extreme in the other direction? Instead of being placid and permissive, will they become excessively severe and even cruel? Will the failure of permissiveness give carte blanche to the sadistic parent who is moved only by his baser, animalistic instincts? Is there a possibility that society may turn back the clock, and maybe all the way back? Even back to the old Mosaic law, when rebellious youth were given something far more terrible than the rod—stoning to death at the city gates?

Solomon did not advocate any such extreme reaction. But he did advocate a return to the rod. Yes, to the rod. This philosopher-king told it like it still is today: "He that spareth his rod hateth his son" (Proverbs 13:24). Solomon would call us to nothing less than a return to corporal punishment.

Solomon was so convinced of the validity of this course that he was not in the least bit intimidated by those who continually prate on the possibility of physical harm to the child. Solomon brushed that argument aside: "For if thou beatest him with the rod, *he shall not die*" (Proverbs 23:13, emphasis added). But how could he afford to be so seemingly callous? Because he had another argument, and one that brings the debate to a swift end: "Thou shalt beat him with the rod, and shalt deliver his soul from hell" (Proverbs 23:14). Even death is a trivial matter and a small price to pay compared with an eternity in hell.

Lest anyone conclude from all this that Solomon advocated indiscriminate and irresponsible corporal punishment, he should think again. Solomon advocated no such thing. The corporal punishment he proposed is buttressed by adequate safeguards. Solomon set specific limits on the administration of punishment.

One limit Solomon emphasized was that the rod must be the *father's rod.* Discipline and punishment must be administered in love, and with parental affection. *"But he that loveth him* chasteneth him" (Proverbs 13:24, emphasis added). Whose hand wields the rod makes all the difference in the world. The father knows his son; he knows of the surging feelings within him and the increasing pressures without. The father knows of the temptation-riddled society in which his son lives; knows of the friends and acquaintances who influence him; knows the climate of his upbringing; knows the very air he breathes. He who wields the rod knows all the circumstances. No one is better qualified than the father to administer the punishment. As the old saying goes, the father "has a firm hand, a fair mind, and a full heart."

For another thing, Solomon stated that the rod should be used "betimes": "But he that loveth him chasteneth him betimes." This word *betimes* is an emphatic word, coming right at the end of the sentence. It tells us that discipline should take place *early,* and in time. The original meaning of the Hebrew word is "with the dawn." You find the same word in Genesis 26:31: "And they rose up betimes in the morning"; and again in Job 24:5: "Behold, as wild asses in the desert, go they forth to their work; rising betimes for a prey." This means that the discipline and punishment of a child should commence at an early age, during the tender years.

This was exactly the program of Susanna Wesley, as she was quoted by Edith Kenyon in *The Life of John Wesley:* "I insist on the conquering of the will of children betimes, because this is the only strong and rational foundation of a religious education without which both precept and example will be ineffectual."

The tragedy too often is that parents have delayed disciplining their children until they are teenagers, and then they find it is too late. By that time their child's will is stubborn, his passions are strong, and his ideas are solidified. He is now angry and rebellious, taking his cue not from his parents, but from some smart-aleck peers who have never had the touch of God upon their lives. Discipline must start "with the dawn."

> I took a piece of living clay
> And gently pressed it day by day;
> I moulded with my pen and art
> A young child's soft and yielding heart.
>
> I came again when years had gone:
> It was a man I looked upon.
> He still the early impressions bore,
> And I could fashion it no more!
>
> AUTHOR UNKNOWN

The parent who neglects the rod fails his child and is guilty of an injustice against him. In what way does he fail his child?

RESULTS OF RELAXED DISCIPLINE

The parent who fails to discipline fails his child by *stunting his moral understanding.* A child expects to be punished for his wickedness. This is the principle he sees functioning in every other department of life. He puts his finger in the fire, and he gets burned. He hits his playmate on the nose, and he gets hit back. But his parents, who through overindulgence fail to discipline him confuse his thinking and warp his understanding. He is confused because he is allowed to get away with his wickedness. On the inside the voice of God is telling him, "Thou shalt not"; but on the outside the voices of his parents are saying, "Forget it." The child, of course, will not comprehend the ramifications of God's moral law; indeed, he may well be unaware of the existence of such a law. But deep within, the child knows there is something wrong somewhere. Such confusion tears the child apart. Intuitively he knows that one cannot sin and get away with it, but that is exactly what his parents allow him to do. Later on in life he will be able to understand things more clearly and know something about the contradiction between the moral law of God and the permissive attitude of his parents. He will then know who was right and who was wrong. But while he is a child he can only understand this moral law in an intuitive and instinctive way.

One writer showed great insight when he said that in a deep, subconscious way, many a boy rebels against society in order to receive the punishment he knows he should have received from his parents. That punishment was not forthcoming from his parents; now it is forthcoming from the law.

Some years ago at the Guelph Correctional Institute, the young lawbreakers there were asked to delve into their backgrounds and come up with a "Code for Parents." How would they like to have seen their parents act toward them? Some of the answers given were shockers—*for the parents.* One answer given by many of the boys was this: "Bug us a little. Be strict and consistent in dishing out discipline. Show us who's boss. It gives us a feeling of security." Another common answer was this: "If you catch us lying, stealing, or being cruel, get tough. When we need punishment, dish it out. But let us know you still love us." And yet another frequently given answer: "Light a candle. Show us the way. Tell us God is not dead, sleeping, or on vacation."

Those kids at Guelph were asking their parents for just one thing: that they act like parents. They understood the wisdom of Solomon better than most fathers and mothers.

He who neglects the rod fails his child by making him *inconsiderate of the needs of others.* The child who is deprived of discipline is allowed to "do his own thing." He is encouraged to say, "I've gotta be me." Follow this philosophy through, and later the child will find himself in the state of the people of Israel in the days of the Judges: doing "that which was right in his own eyes" (Judges 17:6). More often than not, this meant doing what was wrong.

To teach a child to think, "I've gotta be me," is to misunderstand the teaching of the Word of God, and also to misunderstand the meaning of human liberty.

As an example, there is the well-known case of the immigrant who, upon arrival in New York City, punched the nose of the first man he encountered. When the man objected, the immigrant replied: "But this is the land of the free!"

To which the victim responded with firmness: "Remember, mister, your freedom ends where my nose begins!"

God teaches us the same truth: we are not our own, and we should no longer live unto ourselves. Man must be concerned about others and the needs of others, and there is no better time to instill this truth than when a child is young. By firmness and discipline, the truth must be conveyed to him that there are other beings in the world besides himself, and that all those others have rights and privileges, as he has, that need to be respected. A child must be taught that the axis of the universe is not to be confused with the axle of his tricycle.

Dr. Max Rafferty, former state superintendent of public schools in California, said: "Independence and self-reliance are the last things in the world our offspring need to learn. They are positively bristling with these sterling qualities, like so many adolescent porcupines." That is just another way of saying that no man should live unto himself.

He who neglects the rod fails his child by making him *doubt his parents' love and care.* Solomon makes it clear that it is the one who loves the child who should chasten him. "But he that loveth him chasteneth him." In other words, discipline itself is a facet of love, or, if you like, a special expression of love, and children intuitively recognize it.

There were two young boys in a small American town, going out for the evening together. Just as they left the house, one said to the other: "My parents insist that I be home by 10:00 P.M."

To which the other little boy answered: "I wish my parents cared."

Discipline does not have to be justified to the child; he will understand it. Lack of discipline, however, will raise questions within him—questions about his parents' love and concern.

"The spoiled child," said Joseph Parker, "comes to hate the spoiling parent. The child that is wisely chastened comes to love the very hand that used the rod." This is exactly what Solomon was saying: the parent who neglects discipline betrays a lack of love toward his child. Indeed, he put it even stronger: "He that spareth his rod *hateth* his son" (emphasis added).

Listen to Charles Bridges reprimanding those indulgent parents who wink at the vicious habits of their offspring: "Better that the child had been trained in the house of strangers, than that he should thus be the unhappy victim of the cruelty of parental love."

He who neglects the rod fails his child by *depriving him of the wholesomeness and happiness that come from a well-disciplined life.* Discipline, of course, means much more than using the rod; it means purposely depriving the child of many things and denying him many requests so he can learn the true values of life. In this way he is kept unspoiled from excess and indulgence.

Consider the case of a certain seventeen-year-old boy in a midwestern courtroom. He had been caught breaking into a neighborhood house and stealing $6,000 worth of furs and jewelry. He was given a stiff prison sentence. After delivering the sentence, the judge asked to see the boy's father in his chambers. They happened to be next-door neighbors. The father slumped into a chair and, embarrassed, buried his face in his hands. "I don't understand it. His mother and I have given him everything. The boy knows how much we love him. He didn't need the money. Why did he have to steal?"

"That is why I asked you here, Henry," said the judge. "We've known each other long enough for me to speak freely. I'm sorry to say this, but I've seen this coming for a long time. You hit the nail on the head when you said you've given your boy everything. That is the trouble. You've given him too much. You should have been more selfish with the boy!"

That judge could have said the same thing to

many a father in the Bible. He could have said it to Eli, the high priest who indulged his sons and never raised a finger to correct them. Eli lived long enough, however, to see the results of his neglect, both in the untimely death of his sons and in his own grief as a father. "Some parents, like Eli, bring up their children to bring down their house" (George Swinnock).

The judge could have said it to David, the king who could govern a nation better than he could govern his own house. One of his sons became a rapist, and another a murderer. Another son, Adonijah, tried to seize the kingdom, and all because of lack of discipline at home. The Bible states it bluntly: "And his father had not displeased him at any time" (1 Kings 1:6). And, of course, the story of Absalom's treachery is known to all. After his father, David, had indulged his every whim, Absalom repaid him by consorting and conspiring with his father's enemies; ultimately he led an insurrection against David.

By doing everything for their children, parents deprive their children of the ability to do for themselves. The result is that there is a vital ingredient lacking in their children's characters. Instead of wholesomeness of personality, there are feelings of inadequacy and overdependency. Strange as it may seem, discipline contributes to a child's well-being, and ultimately to his happiness. "God's wounds cure, sin's kisses kill," wrote William Gurnall.

He who neglects the rod fails his child by *sowing seeds of distrust in God's Word.* God's Word is explicit on this matter of discipline. If you are a parent and have neglected God's instruction on this point, remind yourself that one day when your child is grown up, he will read the Bible for himself. He will discover at that point that you ignored God's Word in the means you employed in his upbringing. He will realize how you listened to advice given by all sorts of men, but never to the advice given by the Lord Himself.

Bear in mind that God's method is the only method that can ever hope to succeed—yes, even with the rebellious generation of our day. When the methods advanced by psychologists and psychiatrists are proving inadequate; those of educators and teachers, inadequate; those of counselors and modern-day specialists, inadequate; the methods advocated by God's Word do not fail.

Of all the damage done to a child, the most serious is done when seeds of distrust in God's Word are sown in his mind. Parents are to represent God's authority in the home and put God's precepts into practice. Fathers and mothers are called upon to be "the physical arms of the Lord." They are the ones to carry out the Lord's chastisement. If they fail to do this they fail to obey God, and they fail in their responsibility to the child.

Ultimately, the harsh truth has to be admitted: rebellious children indicate rebellious parents. Parents rebel against the Word of God; children rebel against the word of their parents. "As for those parents who will not use the rod upon their children, I pray God He useth not their children as a rod for them" (Thomas Fuller).

START EARLY

The name of Francis Xavier is indelibly impressed on church history as representing a man who believed with passion in the early training of children. He developed a catechism to indoctrinate and capture their young minds and hearts. His famous words are still remembered: "Give me the children until they are seven, and anyone may have them afterwards." He put that statement to work out on the mission fields of India, and in time a multitude of seasoned Catholics were found all over the country.

Xavier was so successful that the Roman Catholic Church adopted his methods, and as a result spread their faith throughout the Far East. Untold millions of heathens were brought into the Roman Catholic fold as a result of his work. Xavier had found a method by which he could instill spiritual truth and discipline into the lives of little children.

John Newton, author of the famous hymn "Amazing Grace," hardly knew his father but was fortunate to be raised by a mother who was a godly woman. She nurtured him in the Christian faith with the aid of Isaac Watts's *Divine Songs Attempted in Easy Language for the Use of Children.* But Newton's mother died when he was seven, and his stepmother proved to be indifferent to religion. He soon learned profanity and ribaldry, went away to sea, entered on a life of extreme dissoluteness, was flogged for desertion, was rejected by friends and family, and finally admitted that the only crime of which he was not guilty was dishonesty. This life-style went on for many years. "But," as one of his biographers stated, "those moral songs and Scripture verses nagged his conscience." John Newton discovered that he could not escape from them, and finally he was converted. In time, he became a great power for God in Olney and, indeed, throughout the English-speaking world. His sermons were anointed of the Lord, and his hymns reached the ends of the earth. As far as John Newton was concerned, those *seven early years had been vital.* Subsequent corruptions were never able to obliterate their impact.

Parents can better train and discipline their children than can any teacher, preacher, or missionary, for parents have an ally on their side. They have natural affection. The secret they have to learn, however, is the need and responsibility to wed this natural affection to parental firmness, and to do so "with the dawn."

Proverbs 25:11
*A word fitly spoken is like apples of gold
in pictures of silver.*

7

ARE WORDS ALL THAT IMPORTANT?

The late Dr. T. T. Shields of Canada once re-marked that we needed a new rescue mission: a rescue mission for fallen words!

We think of words like *propaganda, trip, grass, acid, tea, bread, gay, inoperative,* and *resurrection of the body*–noble words that have had their meanings debased.

> In olden days when people heard
> Some swindler huge had come to grief,
> They used a good old Saxon word,
> And called the man a thief;
> But language such as that today,
> Upon man's tender feeling grates,
> So they look wise, and simply say,
> He re-hy-poth-e-cates.

WRONG IDEAS ABOUT WORDS

We often hear it said that words are *cheap,* but they are not always so. As a matter of fact, there are times when words can cost us dearly, and there are times when we would pay any price to have them re-called. But three things never come back: a spoken word, a sped arrow, and a lost opportunity. The truth of the matter is that some words we have uttered have exacted a very high price—not so much in monetary currency as in the currency of an uneasy conscience, an undying quarrel, or a family feud.

As long as words remain unspoken, we are masters of them; but once spoken, our words master us.

Sometimes it is said that words are *trivial;* but again, this is not always so. Sometimes they are gigantic in the fires they ignite, in the troubles they spawn, and in the crusades they launch. "Syllables govern the world," said John Selden.

The apostle James certainly did not think words were trivial:

> Even so the tongue is a little member, and boasteth great things. Behold, how great a matter a little fire kindleth! And the tongue is a fire, a world of iniquity: so is the tongue among our members, that it defileth the whole body, and setteth on fire the course of nature; and it is set on fire of hell. For every kind of beasts, and of birds, and of serpents, and of things in the sea, is tamed, and hath been tamed of mankind: but the tongue can no man tame; it is an unruly evil, full of deadly poison (James 3:5-8).

A few years ago, a man walked all the way from New York to California. Reporters met him as he arrived on the West Coast and asked if he had ever thought of quitting. "Many times," he replied. They pursued his remark and asked what was the greatest hindrance he encountered. "It wasn't the rushing traffic in the cities," he answered, "nor the blaring horns and screeching brakes of cabs or trucks. It wasn't even those interminable midwestern plains that just went on and on as if they would never end. Nor was it the ice-tipped mountains of the Rockies. It wasn't even the blazing sun over the desert. What almost defeated me over and over again was the sand in my shoes.''[1] Words also may be small like sand, and yet they can be the source of our greatest irritations. They can kill friendships, divide families, and even dissolve marriages.

It has been said that words are *constant*. But again, this is not always the case. Like many other things, they change. Sometimes a word can convey a different meaning in a different culture. There is the famous example of a particular word used in American-Japanese correspondence just before the atom bomb attack on Hiroshima in 1946. The Japanese were forewarned of the attack in the hope that it would pressure them to seek peace. The answer they returned was interpreted in a negative fashion, as "No comment," or "To kill with silence." Later, however, it was explained that this Japanese word could and should have been translated, not as "No comment," but as "We have not discussed it yet." It was not a categorical negative, but "Wait for us to consider it."

Sometimes a word can change its meaning within the same culture, and change its meaning for the worse. This has happened, alas, to many of our fine English words.

There is, for example, the word *gossip*. We read in the New Testament that "They . . . went every where preaching the word" (Acts 8:4). If the translators had been bold enough, they would have used the word *gossip*. "They went every where *gossiping* the word." Today, however, *gossip* is a fallen word. People no longer gossip the Good News about God, but bad news about a neighbor.

Or consider the word *adult*. It used to be an honorable word, full of implications of responsibility and maturity. But how have the mighty fallen! Nowadays, when a child sees the sign "Adults Only," what lurid and unsavory images must leap to his mind. It is either a drinking saloon, a pornographic bookshop, a blue-film theater, or a questionable massage parlor. A child in a London Sunday school class, studying the seventh commandment, shocked his teacher by defining adultery as "that which adults do"!

Then there is the expression, *resurrection of the body*; a noble Christian phrase raised directly from the New Testament and the Apostles' Creed. But the meaning given to it by certain modern, radical revolutionaries is nothing but blasphemy compounded. They use the phrase "resurrection of the body" to sanction sexual license and drug indulgence. They argue that the Puritan ethic has killed the body by denying the gratification of carnal appetites. According to them, glutting our carnal, lustful appetites will resurrect it again!

These are only a few of the many words that have fallen from their original, uncontaminated estate.

WORD POWER

Solomon had a lot to say about words. In Proverbs 15:1 he referred to the *healing power* of words. "A soft answer turneth away wrath: but grievous words stir up anger."

The word *soft* here is not to be equated with weakness or effeminacy, but rather with speech that is marked by modesty and graciousness. The Vulgate translates it as "the gentle, mild tongue." The man whose words are charged with hate and anger may well be overcome by the unexpectedness of a gracious and modest reply. He never anticipates that his lacerating remarks could be answered in such a soothing, healing manner.

A wonderful feature of the Bible is that it gives us not only precepts but examples as well. A good example of this proverb in action is the story of Abigail and

David, in 1 Samuel 25. Abigail was the wise wife of a
foolish husband, Nabal, and a woman who saved her
family from death by her courteous words and gracious behavior. Nabal was rich, but he refused to give
any of his goods to the servants of David during a period of need. He refused to give in spite of all the
kindness David had bestowed upon him on a previous
occasion. Because of this mean and churlish act,
David was angered, and armed four hundred of his
men to execute vengeance on Nabal and his house.
The wise Abigail, however, learned of this and inter-
cepted David before he got to Nabal. By her "soft" answers, her modest attitude, and kind hospitality, she
was able to turn back the sword of the avenger and
save her household.

In this context one is reminded of the Puritan divine John Cotton, of whom it was stated: "He would
not set the beacon of his great soul on fire at the
landing of a little boat."

And there was the famous Curé D'Ars in France,
the lowliest and humblest of all the saints. His fellow
clerics were envious of his sanctity, so they initiated
whisper campaigns against him, smearing his reputation and assassinating his character. They even dubbed
him "God's idiot." Some of them would stand up in
church conferences and falsely accuse him of the most
scurrilous behavior; when they had completed their
accusations, the saintly Curé would arise, and, to
everyone's amazement, agree with their contentions—
even second their motions! In the end, his fellow clerics
came to hate him so much that they drew up a petition to
send to the bishop to have him removed. When that
petition was ready and signed, somehow—before
reaching the bishop's desk—it fell into the hands of the
Curé himself. The lowly saint studied the petition with
the aid of his flickering candle. His eyes became

dimmed with tears as he read what it said about his ignorance, incompetence, and failures. Later, when that
petition reached the bishop's hands, the bishop found
among the signatures that of the Curé D-Ars himself! Is it
any wonder that the names of his persecutors have long
been forgotten, whereas that of the Curé remains a
household word in France?

In Proverbs 15:2 and 17:7, Solomon refers to the
revealing power of words. "The tongue of the wise
useth knowledge aright: but the mouth of fools
poureth out foolishness" (Proverbs 15:2). "Excellent
speech becometh not a fool: much less do lying lips a
prince" (Proverbs 17:7).

A man can be known by his words. Just as dirty
words reveal a dirty mind, so clean words—unless the
man is a hypocrite—reveal a clean mind, and back of
that a clean heart. "For out of the abundance of the
heart the mouth speaketh" (Matthew 12:34). "For as
he thinketh in his heart, so is he" (Proverbs 23:7).

Let no one think that language is unimportant.
Dirty language comes from a dirty inner life, a life
characterized by vile thoughts, sordid desires, and
burning lusts. One is never surprised to find that foul
speech and criminal activity go together. Brutalization
of language and brutalization of life are close
neighbors. Tune in to some of our television plays and
programs and note how hoodlums invariably speak in
obscenities and expletives. Their diction is never a
credit to the nobility of the English language, and
certainly not to the moral sensitivity of decent, law-
abiding citizens. Grunts, abbreviated expletives, and
Anglo-Saxon vulgarities are not the symbols of clean
and honorable living. When you degrade a people's
language, you degrade their life. According to one
authority, both Nazi Germany and Communist Russia
deliberately degraded their people's diction for the

reason that "verbal decencies were barriers to totalitarianism." In the same vein, it could be said that certain moviemakers are contributing to the downfall of democracy and the American way of life by commercializing blasphemy and merchandising dirty speech. A permissive society that allows such things to happen denies its children some of its most basic values, both moral and aesthetic. This happens when a nation trades in its heritage of the Bible, prayer, and worship for smut, obscenity, and vulgarity.

One is aware, of course, that clean language by itself, or education by itself, cannot solve the problems of society. But one thing we do know: such things would lend much encouragement to those who are endeavoring to solve our problems. They would say a resounding amen to Jesus Christ and His ministry in the world. Ultimately, it is only Christ who can change the human heart; when that occurs, a notable feature of the change is that it includes a man's words as well as his actions—his lips as well as his life.

One coal miner known for his lurid and blasphemous language down in the mines was converted during the Welsh Revival of 1904-5. This man later testified: "When I got converted in the revival, I lost 75 percent of my vocabulary!" There is nothing more revealing than words.

When the harlot Pelagia was converted, she gave as her reason, "I have heard the talk of the Christians." This woman of beautiful body but tarnished soul used to frequent the restaurants of Antioch, and while there she would eavesdrop on the conversations of the Christians. On one occasion there was a convocation of bishops in town, and they were sitting in front of the Basilica of Julian when Pelagia passed by. She was "bare of head and shoulder and limb," and riding on an ass. When they saw her, all but one of the bishops turned their faces away in embarrassment. Only Nonnus, the bishop of Edessa, dared to look upon her. He, by divine intuition, recognized the beauty that would sit one day in the presence of God "in judgment of ourselves and our episcopate." Some time later, Pelagia sent Nonnus a note by the hand of one of her servants and reminded him of Christ and the woman of Samaria. How did she know about Christ and the woman of Samaria? "I have heard the talk of the Christians." Pelagia was converted and baptized, and later went to live in a cell on the Mount of Olives. There she remained, devoted to prayer and fasting, until she died. The former harlot became known for her saintliness and deep spirituality.[2] But it all began so casually: a few unknown Christians had been talking in the restaurants of Antioch, and their talk had led her to "the Lamb of God, which taketh away the sin of the world" (John 1:29).

In Proverbs 25:11, Solomon refers to the *appealing power* of words. "A word fitly spoken is like apples of gold in pictures of silver." The figure portrayed was probably an Oriental decoration. Skilled Eastern craftsmen were accustomed to carving fruits in gold and delicately setting them in silver filigree. Such ornaments were expensive, and fit for a king's chamber.

So with words. When they are spoken at the appropriate time, they possess great appeal and winsomeness. That is the time when they are most likely to be heard and acted upon. One day, a word may be dull and pointless; the next day, it is pregnant with purpose and meaning. This is the meaning of the expression used here by Solomon: "Words fitly spoken." Its literal root meaning was "words on wheels." Could anything be more graphic? Today, pedestrian: tomorrow, on wheels. When the right word is spoken at the right time, it has tremendous impact.

If any duty requires this careful use of words, it is the duty of administering a reproof to another. To reprove a Christian brother for a sin he has committed calls for the most delicate handling, both in phraseology and in timing. It is a Christian obligation, of course, and ultimately a sign of our love, to reprove an erring brother; but unless such reproof is done in the right spirit and with the right words, it can accomplish more damage than good. It can harden a man in his sin rather than deliver him from it.

George Swinnock, the Puritan divine, gave excellent advice on this topic when he said: "Reprove compassionately. Soft words and hard arguments do well together. Passion will heat the sinner's blood, but compassion will heal his conscience." And again: "The reprover should have a lion's stout heart, or he will not be faithful, and a lady's soft hand, or he is not like to be successful."

Sometimes it is advisable to reprove a sinner in private, as Paul did on some occasions, so that while convicting a sinner's conscience one does not openly injure his credit. Sometimes it is advisable to administer a reproof indirectly, by ambush rather than by direct frontal attack. Swinnock also said, "Paul, in his sermon to Felix, seemed to shoot at random, not naming any, but his arrow pierced the unrighteous prince to the quick. A wise reprover in this is like a good fencer, who, though he strike one part, yet none that stand by could perceive from his eye, or the carriage of his arm, that he aimed at that more than the rest."

In Proverbs 26:4-5, Solomon refers to the *silencing power* of words. "Answer not a fool according to his folly, lest thou also be like unto him. Answer a fool according to his folly, lest he be wise in his own conceit."

These two verses seem contradictory in their advice. *Paradoxical* would be a better word, however, especially if one gives *paradox* the meaning suggested by Chesterton: "Truth standing on its head to attract attention." This text certainly has that. It may be a little clearer in a later translation: "Do not answer a stupid man in the language of his folly, or you will grow like him; answer a stupid man as his folly deserves, or he will think himself a wise man" (NEB).

Today, the word *folly* may not be strong enough. It conveys mere lack of understanding or dullness of mind—a not-too-serious charge. In the Bible, however, the word *folly* has a much more serious and sinister meaning. There it means "perverseness, depravity, wickedness." That is why the advice is given: "Answer not a fool according to his folly, lest thou also be like unto him." His depravity is such that it may well be contagious, so do not compromise your belief or your language as you answer him. If you do, you may grow to be like him. You can catch his disease, but he will not catch your health.

When you answer a fool, there are two guidelines put forth by Solomon:

1. *Protect yourself.* Do not be tempted to imitate his language and attitude, lest by so doing you degrade yourself to his level.

2. *Correct him.* This you do by reproving him of his folly, and not by pandering to his vanity. "Imitation," said Charles Caleb Coltan, "is the sincerest of flattery." So keep to your own standard, both for his good and your own. Do not imitate him in his perverse and depraved mentality. Jesus said the same thing as Solomon, a thousand years later: "Give not

that which is holy unto the dogs, neither cast ye your pearls before swine" (Matthew 7:6).

Sometimes the best reproof to a fool is silence—silence not as the absence of an answer, but as an answer. That is the kind of answer Jesus gave to Herod when "He answered him nothing" (Luke 23:9). What could have been more eloquent and effective? The silent treatment meted out to the curious and carnal king was far more effective as an instrument of censure than any word Jesus could have uttered. There are times when the sting of silence goes deeper than the scourge of words. Jesus answered the Pharisees in spite of their repugnant self-righteousness; He answered them with some of His most vivid and pungent epithets. He answered Pontius Pilate, although Pilate was sitting in judgment upon Him and would soon hand Him over for execution. But as for Herod, "He answered him nothing." In spite of all his questions and queries—"nothing."

There is something here that could well suggest a foretaste of the judgment to come. The solemnity of divine judgment is such that words are inadequate to convey the sentence: a look, maybe, but no words. Sinner! It is a thousand times better to flinch under the scathing chastisement of God in this world than to face His eternal silence in the next. Can any hell be worse than to be dismissed from the Judge's presence, with the verdict so obvious that it need not be pronounced?

Proverbs 26:17
He that passeth by,
and meddleth with strife belonging not to him,
is like one that taketh a dog by the ears.

8

SHOULD ONE GET INVOLVED?

Nothing is so emphasized today as the virtue of Christian involvement. "Am I my brother's keeper?" This ancient question from the pages of Genesis is receiving a resounding affirmative answer—so much so, that it seems superfluous to even debate the issue. Both liberals and conservatives are agreed that Christians should get involved in the problems and issues of the day. The only disagreement is on the degree of involvement, and sometimes on the nature of the involvement. Provided that by "involvement" we mean what the good Samaritan meant, however, there is no disagreement. Such involvement is a Christian responsibility, and is therefore applicable to all Christians everywhere. To deny this would be to assume a distorted view of the Christian faith and a callous indifference to human need. As a matter of fact, it would be tantamount to deny the gospel itself.

A glaring example of indifference was furnished to us a few years ago. The incident happened in an apartment building in New York City and received wide coverage in the news media. A man was attacked by a gang of hoodlums while sitting in his apartment. Lighter fluid was thrown into his face and then poured over his body. He was then set on fire. His screams were so loud that they were heard all over the building. He died in his apartment, and not one of his neighbors—not a single one—went to his aid. One neighbor admitted he had heard the screams and decided to turn up the volume on his television! He did not want to get involved.

I have often wondered if any Christians lived in that apartment building, and if so, how they felt in church the following Sunday. What if the lesson had been Luke 10:25-37? Or what if the choir had sung "Make Me a Blessing"? There can be no question about one's duty in such a situation. To help would be only human, not to mention Christian.

However, there are situations in which the question of involvement is not so easy to answer, situations in which involvement has not been beneficial either to the party in need or the party who got involved. How often have we reprimanded ourselves for getting involved in issues and situations that backfired, when we have said with belated wisdom, "I wish I had never gotten involved"?

It was with the later-regretted kind of involvement that Solomon deals in chapter 26 of Proverbs—the kind of involvement that is unwise, or even clearly wrong. Solomon calls it involvement in the *strife* of others; not in their suffering, but in their strife. He is not referring to the man who is anxious to help others when there is genuine need but to the man who enjoys prying and interfering in the affairs of others. He does not refer to the busy man but to the busybody, the man who has itching ears to know everything and an itching tongue to exaggerate everything, the man who gets involved solely for his own perverted pleasure. Such is the man of whom Solomon speaks here—the man who revels in the strife of others.

In Proverbs 25:8, Solomon warns us not to engage hastily in our *own* strife, let alone in the strife of others. "Go not forth hastily to strive, lest thou know not what to do in the end thereof, when thy neighbour hath put thee to shame." Paul issues the same warning, and then proceeds to classify strife in the same category as adultery, idolatry, witchcraft, heresy, murder, and so on (Galatians 5:19-21).

Many Christians (some inadvertently) have found themselves embroiled in the strife of others, only to discover that they had to bear a portion of the blame themselves. Like a man caught in a maelstrom, they were caught and unable to get out of it. And what was worse, in the process of trying to get out they succeeded only in getting deeper and deeper into the strife.

It is obvious that when a Christian gets involved in the strife of others, he is not going to escape unscathed. He will invariably have to bear part of the blame himself, and sometimes the brunt of the blame. No one is convinced when that Christian tries to justify himself by resorting to a lot of silly, sanctimonious statements such as: "This is the particular cross that God would have me bear"; or "This is what Christian discipleship means—being numbered with the transgressors." Such statements are spurious. The cross he is referring to is not the Lord's doing at all, but his own doing; it is something he has brought on himself by his own foolish meddling. How wise was the comment of Charles Bridges: "A wide difference is made between 'suffering as a busy-body, and suffering as a Christian.'"

WHAT'S THE DIFFERENCE?

One is aware, of course, that the line between assisting and interfering is not always clearly drawn.

Nor is the line clearly drawn between a dispute and strife. When does a dispute become strife? Is it right to get involved in a dispute, but not in strife?

Solomon, in his God-given wisdom, was aware of this distinction. That is the reason, I believe, that he chose his terms so meticulously. Note the three terms that he used. Look first at his choice of the term "strife." The Hebrew word used by Solomon is a strong word and carries with it the idea of "kindling a fire." Read Isaiah 50:11 and you find the same word being used: "Behold, all ye that *kindle a fire*, that compass yourselves about with sparks" (emphasis added). It should be clearly noted that getting involved in such strife is not the same as offering assistance to a neighbor who has been viciously attacked by an intruder. Meddling in others' strife refers rather to a man who irresponsibly interferes in the affairs of other people, and by so doing kindles a veritable bonfire; and if that were not enough, he keeps adding fuel to it.

Notice second Solomon's choice of the term "meddleth." This word spells out the motive of the man who involves himself. His motive is not to give help; rather, it is to meddle in and aggravate the situation. Such a motive reminds one of the Welsh proverb, *Annoeth cicio nyth cacwn* (It is unwise to kick a hornet's nest). This is exactly what happens when a man meddles in the affairs of others: he succeeds only in aggravating the issue and giving it extra publicity in the bargain. Instead of the strife being contained, it is enlarged and extended.

Third, consider Solomon's choice of the term "he that passeth by." The one who thus involves himself is obviously not a neighbor or an acquaintance, but a complete stranger who does not even know the people concerned. And if he does not know the people, how can he possibly know the cause and nature of the strife between them? He is just a passerby. It is more than probable that when he is done with his meddling, the people will never see him again. He, of all people, should have left matters alone.

GUIDELINES FOR INVOLVEMENT

To help us avoid becoming involved in such unwise and inglorious conduct, let us be directed by two guidelines.

The precepts of Scripture. Solomon warns us in Proverbs, "He that passeth by, and meddleth with strife belonging not to him, is like one that taketh a dog by the ears." The same warning was echoed by Paul when he told the believers in Rome: "For wherein thou judgest another, thou condemnest thyself" (Romans 2:1). And the same warning came again by a greater one than Solomon and Paul: "Judge not, that ye be not judged" (Matthew 7:1).

This is not to say that a Christian cannot be critical or express an adverse opinion of others. What is condemned is the Christian who assumes the role of a judge, and by his limited knowledge and judgmental attitude proceeds to condemn a fellow believer, even to the point of meddling in his affairs. Such a Christian's judgment, which is frequently based on prejudice rather than principle, may well be wrong; his meddling is invariably wrong.

Another thing that happens when a man takes upon himself the functions of a judge is that he sets a standard by which he himself will be judged. He may well find that his judgment and condemnation of others will boomerang. Let us take an example. Suppose a man decides to visit the Sistine Chapel in Rome, and once there he begins to gaze at that famous ceiling with all its priceless masterpieces of

Michaelangelo. He then comes out and comments to a friend, "What a waste of good paint!" Such a remark would tell you nothing about Michaelangelo but a great deal about the man who made the remark. He did not succeed in condemning Michaelangelo but only in condemning himself. Or suppose a man went to listen to Beethoven's Fifth Symphony, and came out and said, "What a lot of noise!" He would be condemning not Beethoven but himself.

In the Bible we read, "Jesus stood before the governor" (Matthew 27:11). Jesus stood there, judged and condemned by Pilate. In a deeper and more permanent sense, however, it was Pilate who was judged and condemned by Jesus. G. Campbell Morgan was right when he suggested that the verse could well be rewritten: "And the governor stood before Jesus."

Likewise with Judas, who took it upon himself to sell Christ to His enemies, but discovered by so doing that he had only succeeded in selling himself.

> Men by themselves are priced,
> Judas for thirty pieces
> Sold himself, not Christ.
>   HESTER H. CHOLMONDELEY

The practice of Christ. Christ never flinched from condemning unrighteousness and injustice wherever He found it, and yet one of the abiding mysteries of His ministry is this: when specific cases were referred to Him for judgment, He declined to interfere. He would not pronounce judgment on the person brought to Him. Although He would condemn wrong unhesitatingly, at the same time He would not take sides in individual cases.

Samuel Chadwick gave an example of this in one of his sermons. He referred to Luke 12:13-14, in which a man came to Jesus, claiming he had been treated unfairly and unjustly by his brother. He believed his rights had been denied. "Master, speak to my brother, that he divide the inheritance with me." By bringing his case to Christ, the Preacher of righteousness, the man was sure he would have an impartial hearing and judgment. But what did he find? Christ heard his case all right, but to his amazement, He refused to arbitrate. Indeed, Christ not only refused to arbitrate and pronounce judgment, but He deliberately rebuked the man for bringing the case to Him in the first place! "Man, who made me a judge or a divider over you?" This sort of reaction on the part of Christ was one of the inexplicable things in His ministry. He would preach judgment and yet refuse to pass judgment in specific cases.

Why should this be? I can think of only one answer: Christ came into the world to establish a kingdom that was spiritual and universal. "My kingdom is not of this world" (John 18:36). Because of this, His tenets are not local precepts but universal principles. Therefore, when He deals with specific cases, the judgment He delivers is not to be understood as something personal and individual, but as something universal and everlasting. Having delivered the judgment, however, it is then up to the individual concerned to apply the judgment to himself. This does not mean that Christ was not interested in individual cases, nor that He was insensitive to social injustices. Rather it means that His mission was to lay down universal judgments; He leaves the application of such judgments to the persons concerned.

That was not all He did. Christ did something more; as a matter of fact, He did the most positive and effective thing any person could do. *Christ attacked sin by saving the sinner.* The whole weight of His ministry was in this direction. He would change men

themselves, so that they in turn could change their
situations. This is a far more profound solution to social evils than merely to holler for one's rights. In the
words of Samuel Chadwick, Christ came "to correct
the dispositions of men rather than to secure their
rights."

Christ built for us a glorious edifice on the foundation of wisdom laid down by Solomon. Rather than
get involved in any sort of strife between two brothers,
Christ got down to the root of the matter, proceeded to
give it due exposure, and then pointed out the solution. In the particular case in Luke 12:13-14, He un-
covered the root cause of the strife between the two
brothers: covetousness. Both brothers were eager to
multiply possessions. Then, having exposed the root
cause, Christ proceeded to issue the universal principle of judgment that is applicable to all men
everywhere (including, of course, the two brothers):
"A man's life consisteth not in the abundance of the
things which he possesseth" (Luke 12:15).

What lesson should the followers of Christ derive
from all this? Is it not that they should be actively engaged in issues that call for assistance and mercy,
while at the same time shunning all issues of strife
and interference, seeing that such things only lead to
a judgmental spirit?

THE QUESTION OF RIGHTS

The lesson about meddling in strife applies not
only to our involvement in the strife of others, but also
to our involvement in our own strifes—strifes with
which we are personally and directly concerned. Let's
take one example: should a Christian defend himself
when he has been openly and publicly maligned by
others? Or should he remain silent and by so doing
minimize the amount of strife and friction engen-

dered? In other words, does a Christian stand up for his rights, or does he not?

It is obvious that a Christian has rights like other citizens and is lawfully entitled to stand up for them. The question is, however, whether it is expedient for him to do so. Many a Christian has been severely exercised on this very issue. Should he answer his accusers and defend himself against them, or should he patiently and quietly endure it? Should he retaliate vigorously or assume a discreet silence?

Most Christians would agree that there can be no dogmatic answer to this question, but that every man should respond according to the light of his own conscience. It can be added, however, that the more spiritual and mature believers have generally acted on this principle: when the accusations involve the work of the Lord, and are thus liable to harm that work, a defense should be made publicly. Silence in such a situation could be detrimental to the gospel and the furtherance of the Lord's work. But when the accusations concern only the believer personally, with no direct bearing on the Lord's work, then the more excellent way of the saints has been to remain silent. The saints have been satisfied to leave their defense with Him who knoweth all things. "Vengeance is mine; I will repay, saith the Lord" (Romans 12:19). It is true that such a position has often been misconstrued and has frequently led to much suffering and sacrifice, but it is a price that the saints have paid gladly.

I have used the word "gladly" deliberately in this context for this reason: as far as the saints are concerned, suffering and sacrifice are never regarded as negative virtues. Rather, they are interpreted as positive and effective forms of ministry. Experience has taught the saints that the times when they have been called upon to suffer and sacrifice in the work of the

Lord have turned out to be the times of their greatest
triumphs. They have learned that a grain of wheat has
to die if it is to bring forth fruit.

The son of Adoniram Judson was aware of this
truth when he spoke about his famous father's martyrdom in Burma. He claimed that his father accomplished more for God by his death than by all his life;
more by his sacrifice at the end than by his lifetime of
service. Then he added this profound truth: "If a man
has success without sacrifice, it means that someone
has sacrificed before him. If a man sacrifices without
success, it means that someone will succeed after
him."

The same could be said of young David Brainerd,
who worked so strenuously among the Indian tribes of
New England. His ministry was cut short after only a
few years by severe tuberculosis. He died in the home
of Jonathan Edwards, to whose daughter Jerusha he
was engaged to be married.

> Soon after Brainerd died Jonathan Edwards published
> an account of the life of the young man, together with
> his diary. The book so revealed Brainerd's character
> and dedication that it became a powerful influence on
> many lives on behalf of missions—even to this day. As
> one historian put it, "David Brainerd dead was a more
> potent influence for the missionary cause in general
> than was David Brainerd alive."[1]

True success is invariably tied to sacrifice. This is
why the saints never regard sacrifice as a negative
virtue. To them it is the highest form of service and
the most certain form of success. Is it any wonder that
Ignatius cried out in the hour of his martyrdom: "Let
me be ground with the teeth of wild beasts, if I may be
God's pure wheat."

No, Jesus never stood up for His rights. Not once
did He demand privileges, and not once did He claim
prerogatives. He could have done so, but He chose not

to. Have you ever wondered what would have happened if He had done so? Suppose He had demanded His rights and insisted on His options? If He had, there obviously would have been no cross, and no hope for us.

Proverbs 25:5
Take away the wicked from before the king,
and his throne shall be established
in righteousness.

Proverbs 25:2
It is the glory of God to conceal a thing:
but the honour of kings is to search out a matter.

Proverbs 17:7
Excellent speech becometh not a fool:
much less do lying lips a prince.

9

ARE THERE DIFFERENT STANDARDS FOR LEGISLATORS?

It has been well said that a Christian has a threefold duty toward the state: to pray, to pay, and to obey.

To Pray. Paul told us in 1 Timothy 2:2 that prayers should be made "for kings, and for all that are in authority; that we may lead a quiet and peaceable life in all godliness and honesty."

Those who are in positions of authority certainly need special prayer, if only for the reason that they face greater temptations and are more prone to solipsism. Moral and spiritual dangers to which they are exposed can well shipwreck them for time and eternity. No doubt many a Christian ruler has succumbed to these dangers not only because he himself was weak, but also because Christian people failed to uphold him in prayer. They were readier to join in the public witch-hunt than to engage in private intercession at the throne of grace.

There are times, of course, when it is not easy to pray for those in authority over us, particularly if they belong to a different political party or if they advocate

policies contrary to our own. Former Senator Harold
Hughes of Iowa referred to this kind of dilemma during the Watergate crisis. He told of his uneasiness in
having to criticize the president by day and pray for
him by night. It is not easy to be a man's friend on our
knees and his enemy on our feet. But the injunction of
Scripture remains, that prayer should be made for *all*
in authority, be it easy or not.

It certainly was not easy in Paul's day. The man
who wore the imperial purple at that time was Nero, a
veritable monster of iniquity. Yet Paul exhorted Timothy that "supplications, prayers, intercessions,
and giving of thanks, be made for all men . . . and for
all that are in authority" (1 Timothy 2:1-2).

To Pay. The Scriptures do not hesitate on this
matter, either. They tell us that when the state decrees, Christians should pay; and what is more, Christians should pay *what* the state decrees.

Here again, Christians find themselves in a dilemma. Is it right not only to pray for, but to pay to a
state that acts contrary to one's beliefs and advocates
policies that are unacceptable to a Christian conscience? This was the thrust of the question sprung by
the Pharisees on Jesus. They asked Him: "Is it lawful
to give tribute unto Caesar, or not?"

Jesus, of course, was aware of their cunning and
perversity: "Why tempt ye me, ye hypocrites?" He
then asked for a penny and pointedly inquired,
"Whose is this image and superscription?"

They told Him, "Caesar's."

Then came the Lord's answer, an answer to them
and to us: "Render therefore unto Caesar the things
which are Caesar's; and unto God the things that are
God's" (Matthew 22:17-21).

If this was His answer concerning a ruler like
Caesar, then most certainly it would be His answer

concerning any and every ruler. As we know well, Caesar's policies were objectionable to every Jew in Palestine; worse than that, Caesar was a pagan; and even worse again, he was a pagan who claimed to be divine and never hesitated to teach the people to honor him as such. But in spite of all that, Christ insists: "Render therefore unto Caesar the things which are Caesar's."

To Obey. Again the Scriptures are clear. Paul tells us in Romans 13:1-4:

> Let every soul be subject unto the higher powers. For there is no power but of God: the powers that be are ordained of God. Whosoever therefore resisteth the power, resisteth the ordinance of God: and they that resist shall receive to themselves damnation. For rulers are not a terror to good works, but to the evil. Wilt thou then not be afraid of the power? do that which is good, and thou shalt have praise of the same: For he is the minister of God to thee for good. But if thou do that which is evil, be afraid; for he beareth not the sword in vain: for he is the minister of God, a revenger to execute wrath upon him that doeth evil.

And in Titus 3:1, Paul tells us:

> Put them in mind to be subject to principalities and powers, to obey magistrates, to be ready to every good work.

The primary function of the state is to restrain the forces of evil and to see to it that in no way are they encouraged or legalized.

Here again, Christians face a dilemma. Are there not occasions when a Christian would be justified in disobeying those higher powers? Are there not times and seasons when civil disobedience would be the will of Christ, rather than a timid and pathetic conformity? The answer is not easy, and even the saints disagree. I believe the Scriptures teach us that there is *one* occasion when disobedience to the state would be justified, one occasion when a Christian could rightly say no to the higher powers. That occasion comes when the state has failed to fulfill its God-given and God-ordained function. The state, we are taught, is to be a terror not to good works but to evil works. Suppose the position were reversed, and the state became a terror to good works and an encourager of evil works? What then? I believe that in that very act the state would disqualify itself as a higher power ordained of God. That being the case, Christians would no longer be bound to obedience. They would be free, as the apostles were free, to say: "We ought to obey God rather than men" (Acts 5:29).

Although it is true that the Scriptures refer to the state as "the higher power," the Christian is always aware that there is another power—the highest power. And the highest has preeminence over the higher; the God of the minister over the minister of God.

There is another fact that also should be borne in mind: the God who ordained the higher powers can also remove such powers if it be His will. As Daniel reminds us, God not only sets up kings, but He removes them as well (Daniel 2:21). It is no wonder that the unhappy Mary, Queen of Scots, said that she feared the prayers of John Knox more than an army of twenty thousand men. When a Christian is dissatisfied with the state and finds that it is not fulfilling God's intentions for it, it is his duty to pray to God that the rulers and politicians who govern that state be removed from office. This recourse to prayer is the most powerful weapon in the Christian's arsenal, for God is never apathetic to His people's requests. If only our modern-day politicians, senators, and congressmen believed this. If only they were more afraid of the faithful and their prayers than of the Gallup pollsters and their statistics.

RULES FOR RULERS

Concerning those who rule over us, Solomon had much advice to offer.

First, rulers should secure *truthful aides.* "Take away the wicked from before the king, and his throne shall be established in righteousness" (Proverbs 25:5).

A king, not being omniscient, is dependent most of the time on aides and advisers that surround him. He thus becomes vulnerable to their particular prejudices. Because of this, he is advised to exercise every care in the appointment of such aides, and to take swift action to remove such aides whenever their advice proves false and corrupt. Failure to take such action will damage the king's reputation, and may even bring down his house. Aides wield great power, but little responsibility. They take chances and remain unaccountable. A king has to be on guard, for his reputation is in their hands.

History abounds with examples of good rulers having gone down to destruction, not because of any inherent wickedness of their own, nor because of any conspiratorial action of their enemies, but because of unwise and unworthy friends that surrounded them. Some of those aides failed their masters by directly planning against them, but many more failed them by becoming mere flatterers and sycophants, hiding the unpleasant truth. The advice of William Secker is as germane in the twentieth century as it was in the seventeenth: "It was the saying of a heathen, though not a heathenish saying, 'That he that would be good, must either have a faithful friend to instruct him, or a watchful enemy to correct him.'"

Solomon likewise reminds all rulers, "A wise king scattereth the wicked, and bringeth the wheel over them" (Proverbs 20:26). A wise king cleanses his court from the influence of all evil aides, and by so doing safeguards his throne and dynasty. Solomon's father, King David, spelled it out even more clearly:

> I will set no wicked thing before mine eyes: I hate the work of them that turn aside; it shall not cleave to me. A froward heart shall depart from me: I will not know a wicked person. Whoso privily slandereth his neighbour, him will I cut off: him that hath an high look and a proud heart will not I suffer. Mine eyes shall be upon the faithful of the land, that they may dwell with me: he that walketh in a perfect way, he shall serve me. He that worketh deceit shall not dwell within my house: he that telleth lies shall not tarry in my sight (Psalm 101:3-7).

King Asa was a good example of this precept being put into practice. He was the Old Testament king who removed his own mother from office because she was an evil influence in the court (2 Chronicles 15:16). Nehemiah, another good example, rebuked a member of the high priest's family and dismissed him from the Temple. Those men of God put into practice the wisdom of the Word of God, and by so doing ensured the success of their work.

Second, rulers should search out *the whole truth.* "It is the glory of God to conceal a thing: but the honour of kings is to search out a matter" (Proverbs 25:2).

Here Solomon draws a contrast between the divine King of heaven and the human kings of earth. The glory of the divine King is to conceal; and this He does so successfully that even His choicest servants are forced to conclude, "Verily thou art a God that hidest thyself" (Isaiah 45:15).

Solomon reiterated this truth in 1 Kings 8:12: "The LORD said that he would dwell in the thick darkness." And the psalmist returned frequently to this same theme: "He made darkness his secret place; his pavilion round about him were dark waters and thick clouds of the skies" (Psalm 18:11). "Thy righteousness is like the great mountains; thy judgments are a great deep" (Psalm 36:6).

Normally, things are concealed from us because they are:

1. *too small to be seen.* But God is too great to be seen.
2. *too far away to be seen.* But God is too near to be seen. In the words of Tennyson, "He is nearer than breath, And closer than hands and feet."
3. *too dark to be seen.* But God dwells in too much light to be seen. His light is such that it blinds us. "Dwelling in the light which no man can approach unto; whom no man hath seen, nor can see" (1 Timothy 6:16).

Yes, there are occasions when God does purposely conceal Himself from us. And there are occasions when we want to see too much; and not only to see too much, but we want to hear too much; yes, and to know too much. Not satisfied with merely seeing the ark, we want to pry into it; not satisfied to know that the Lord is coming back, we want to know when and where; not satisfied to accept the mystery of the faith, we want it untied and unraveled. We would do well to emulate Bishop Hall: "I leave God's secrets to Himself. It is happy for me that God makes me of His court though not of His council."

For the kings of the earth, however—legislators, magistrates, rulers, and governors—virtue lies in the opposite direction. Their task is not to cover up, but rather to search out the truth. Rulers are limited in knowledge and wisdom, so they are bidden to search out all the avenues of truth available. No stone should be left unturned, and no testimony unscrutinized. It is not enough to know the truth; they must know the whole truth.

This standard of truth was much higher and more rigorously applied in Old Testament days than it is in our country today. To convict a criminal in those days demanded a far greater degree of certainty. Today, according to our judicial system, the proof required has to be "beyond reasonable doubt." If it meets that requirement, it suffices. But in ancient Israel the proof had to be tantamount to certainty. Before judgment could be passed, the case had to be investigated fully: every lead followed, every fact ascertained, every doubt removed. It is spelled out in Deuteronomy 17:4: "And it be told thee, and thou hast heard of it, and enquired diligently, and, behold, it be true, and the thing certain." That is not a case of no "reasonable" doubt, but of no doubt at all. Rulers are told to search out the full truth.

Third, rulers should always *speak the truth and nothing else.* "Excellent speech becometh not a fool: much less do lying lips a prince" (Proverbs 17:7).

It is an old question but perennially relevant: Should the truth be told on each and every occasion? In other words, are there occasions, however rare, when a lie could be justified? What of the man who tells a lie to save another person's life? This was the dilemma of Corrie ten Boom. If she told the truth, that there were Jews hidden in her father's house, she would have been an accomplice of the Nazis, and would have contributed to the Jews' death in the gas chambers of Ravensbruck. In such a situation, should a lesser evil be committed in order to avoid a much greater evil? It is never an easy question to answer.

What about the dilemma of the Bible smuggler? If he tells the truth at the frontier, all his Bibles will be confiscated, and the saints behind the Iron and Bamboo curtains will be deprived of the precious Word of God. What is he to do?

It is no wonder that many of the other religions of the world hesitate and hedge on this issue. Indeed, some religions plainly teach that there are certain specific occasions when lies are permitted. The Muslim religion, for example, allows two occasions when a person may lie and not be guilty of sin. Both occasions, incidentally, are restricted to women. A woman may tell a lie to save a life, and she may tell a lie during times of war. The Hindu religion goes further and allows five occasions when a person may tell a lie and remain sinless. The permissible lies are in connection with marriage, gratifying one's lust, saving one's life, protecting one's property, and benefiting a Hindu holy man.

What of the Christian faith? Does it allow exceptions? It allows exceptions to the law of the Sabbath and the law against killing, but what of the law concerning telling the truth? Does that law allow exceptions? No, it does not. Scripture is dogmatic on this issue: there is no occasion when a liar can be considered sinless. A lie is a sin on every occasion. "These six things doth the LORD hate: yea, seven are an abomination unto him: a proud look, *a lying tongue . . .*" (Proverbs 6:16-17, emphasis added). "Lying lips are abomination to the LORD: but they that deal truly are his delight" (Proverbs 12:22). Scripture is adamant that there is no exception to this rule.

That being the case, what then is the position of the Christian brother who tells a lie to save another brother from certain death? What of the Christian believer who purposely chooses a lesser evil to be free from the guilt of a greater evil? We are not even thinking in terms of the believer's own fate, but in terms of the fate of another human being. Again, the answer of Scripture is no. A liar is never sinless.

Such an answer, however, would be incomplete if one were not to add a qualifying statement. Although a lie is always a sin, there are certain specific occasions when it is more in accord with the spirit of the Christian faith to tell a lie, and to repent of it afterward, than to passively allow a greater evil to be perpetrated. Do not misunderstand: the lie is still a sin, and still needs to be repented and forgiven, but it is an infinitely lesser guilt to bear than to acquiesce in a greater sin and be responsible for calamitous repercussions.

A DUAL STANDARD?

In view of the above discussion about lying, is it right to assume that rulers and public officials who lie in the national interest are absolved from guilt? After all, they are not lying for their own sake, but for their country's sake. Can such lies be justified? Even Plato allowed for princes to lie as long as it was done for the public good. And today, with international politics demanding such expertise and sophistication, surely the national interest takes precedence over any private or personal scruple. But again the verdict of the Bible is adamant: a lie is a sin. Nothing can possibly alter that fact. What is more, the Bible goes further and claims that a lie is an even greater sin when it is committed by a ruler or other person in authority. A higher standard is always required of such people. "Excellent speech becometh not a fool: much less do lying lips a prince" (Proverbs 17:7). And again: "Righteous lips are the delight of kings; and they love him that speaketh right" (Proverbs 16:13).

King Louis IX of France was closer to the biblical position on this question than Plato. King Louis said, "If truth be banished from the rest of the world, it ought to be found in the breast of princes."

You may well ask why this should be. Why should God demand a higher standard from our governors and legislators than from ordinary people? The best answer to that is to let Scripture speak for itself: "For unto whomsoever much is given, of him shall be much required" (Luke 12:48).

It is not without cause that we are exhorted to pray for these men. The standard is so demanding, the expectation so high, and the flesh so powerful that few of them ever make it. It is no wonder that Buchanan (tutor to the young King James I) when on his deathbed sent a message to his royal pupil that "he was going to a place to which few kings and princes ever came."

The same high standard of honesty applies to us as Christian believers, and rightly so. God expects more from us than from the unredeemed masses. A sin in a saint is always a more heinous crime and a more serious matter than a sin in an unsaved sinner. And if you should ask why, we answer again: "For unto whomsoever much is given, of him shall be much required" (Luke 12:48).

This is why a sin committed in the Temple was always considered a greater sin than the same sin committed at home, or outside in the world. The Temple was a consecrated place, and thus a greater holiness was required. Therefore, concluded William Gurnall: "The saint is a consecrated person, and by acts of unrighteousness he profanes God's temple; the sin of another is theft, because he robs God of the glory due to Him; but the sin of a saint is sacrilege, because he robs God of that which is devoted to Him in an especial manner."

Thomas Watson rendered the same verdict: "For the wicked to sin, there is no other expected from them; swine will wallow in the mire; but when sheep do so, when the godly sin, that redounds to the dishonour of the Gospel: 'By this deed thou hast given great occasion to the enemies of the Lord to blaspheme.'"

Proverbs 6:6-11

Go to the ant, thou sluggard; consider her ways, and be wise: which having no guide, overseer, or ruler, provideth her meat in the summer, and gathereth her food in the harvest. How long wilt thou sleep, O sluggard? when wilt thou arise out of thy sleep? Yet a little sleep, a little slumber, a little folding of the hands to sleep: so shall thy poverty come as one that travelleth, and thy want as an armed man.

Proverbs 12:27

The slothful man roasteth not that which he took in hunting.

Proverbs 19:24

A slothful man hideth his hand in his bosom, and will not so much as bring it to his mouth again.

Proverbs 20:4

The sluggard will not plow by reason of the cold; therefore shall he beg in harvest, and have nothing.

Proverbs 24:30-34

I went by the field of the slothful, and by the vineyard of the man void of understanding; and, lo, it was all grown over with thorns, and nettles had covered the face thereof, and the stone wall thereof was broken down. Then I saw, and considered it well: I looked upon it, and received instruction. Yet a little sleep, a little slumber, a little folding of the hands to sleep: so shall thy poverty come as one that travelleth; and thy want as an armed man.

10

IS WORK JUST ANOTHER FOUR-LETTER WORD?

A young man confided in me a few years ago and claimed that God had directed him *not* to work but to live on welfare. In this way he had more time to witness for the Lord! And with the added felicity of the state footing the bill!

Only the tragedy of the situation kept it from being farcical. Here was a young man who to all appearances was sincere, but who in fact was nothing but a sophisticated, religious hobo. He was guilty of debasing Christian truth in order to justify his own indolence—a glaring example of spurious spiritual reasoning used to cover up carnality of the worst kind.

His case may well be an extreme example, but there is no denying the fact that there are many Christians who unconsciously adopt this attitude, and by so doing succumb to the indolence of their nature. If they can find a good reason for avoiding work, they will use it. That is a far cry from the attitude of Isaac Watts:

> In works of labour or of skill,
> I would be busy too;
> For Satan finds some mischief still
> For idle hands to do.

Such indolence is also a far cry from the old Puritan maxim: "Agenda is as important as Credenda."

Solomon dealt with this problem in the book of Proverbs, returning to it many times. He used a variety of metaphors and allegories to discredit sloth and uphold the virtues of work and diligence. Let's study a few of his examples.

TOTAL SLOTH

> Go to the ant, thou sluggard; consider her ways, and be wise: which having no guide, overseer, or ruler, provideth her meat in the summer, and gathereth her food in the harvest. How long wilt thou sleep, O sluggard? when wilt thou arise out of thy sleep? Yet a little sleep, a little slumber, a little folding of the hands to sleep: So shall thy poverty come as one that travelleth, and thy want as an armed man (Proverbs 6:6-11).

Here is a case of total sloth. Seneca, the heathen philosopher, advised, "It is a shame not to learn morals from the small animals." The Bible goes further and marks certain areas in which we can learn from all animals, small and large. Many times in Scripture a truth is hammered home by comparing a man's actions with those of the animal world. The comparison is usually unfavorable: the ox and the ass reprove us of our *ingratitude* (Isaiah 1:3); the stork, turtle, crane, and swallow of our *inattention* (Jeremiah 8:7); the fowls of the air of our *anxiety* (Matthew 6:26); and the sparrow of our *fear and alarm* (Matthew 10:29-31). Our Lord sighed aloud and wept over the holy city. "O Jerusalem, Jerusalem, thou that killest the prophets, and stonest them which are sent unto thee, how often would I have gathered thy children together, even as a hen gathereth her chickens under her wings, and ye would not" (Matthew 23:37).

Back in Proverbs, man's sloth is held out in contrast to the industry of the ants. We are told how the ants plan and make provision for the day of need. They are the epitome of industry as they go about gathering their food at harvesttime. This they do, said Solomon, without any outside help or apparent command. They have no guide, overseer, or ruler. There is no one they can turn to for assistance; no one to plan their work schedule; and no one to be accountable to at the day's end.

How different is man—the highest being in God's order of creation. Man is too often a spiritual sluggard, using his reason to invent excuses. He does this in spite of the fact that God has supplied him with a host of aids. He has the voice of conscience; the canon of Scripture; preachers and teachers without number; and a heavenly ruler to whom he is accountable.

In spite of all this, many Christians are slothful, sleeping away the opportunities of grace. Their faith has become an anemic passivity, with no drive and no diligence to accomplish anything for God. The only motto that appeals to them is: "Let go, and let God." Their logic is this: the welfare program looks after our physical needs, and God looks after our spiritual needs, so from the cradle to the grave, and beyond the grave, we are all right. This is another example of a glorious truth being theologically manipulated.

I recall a Christian brother rising in a conference on one occasion and going to great lengths to condemn a fellow believer for being overzealous and overindustrious in the Lord's work. This was the censure he administered: "Sure he never misses a church service, and never misses an evangelistic rally, and never misses any kind of religious get-together." Then came the cut at the jugular: "But it is mere *activism*."

We are aware, of course, of the sense in which religious activism is to be discounted and even condemned. This is the activism that has as its goal the earning of one's salvation. Such activism is practiced by those people who engage in various social and religious activities with the sole aim of securing a ticket to heaven. Such misguided souls do exist. But in our attempt to discredit such a practice, there is a grave danger of overreacting and condemning all religious activism per se. Activism as a means of salvation is certainly to be condemned, but activism issuing from salvation is to be expected and, indeed, encouraged. As a matter of fact, if there is no activism, then our salvation should be suspect. Religious pursuits like church attendance, Bible conferences, evangelistic rallies, skid row missions, wars on poverty, and feeding the hungry should be the norm for the born-again believer. To deny this is to make nonsense of spiritual duties and disciplines; indeed, in some instances it should be interpreted as a subtle and convenient cloak for plain sloth.

Jesus was certainly an activist. How else could one understand statements like: "The zeal of thine house hath eaten me up" (John 2:17); and "My Father worketh hitherto, and I work" (John 5:17). And does He not bid us time and again to strive, to labor, to seek, and to knock? Why? Because these verbs pulsate with activism.

There can be no denying the fact that in the eyes of God, indolence is a sin, and a great sin. It is not a mere misfortune or peccadillo, but a breach of God's commandment.

A man's salvation is the work of the Lord, and totally of the Lord. At the same time, it is a salvation that results in human activity. The believer receives his salvation from the Lord, but then he works out his salvation "with fear and trembling" (Philippians 2:12).

PARTIAL SLOTH

> The slothful man roasteth not that which he took in hunting (Proverbs 12:27).

This is partial sloth. The example here is of a man who is not totally slothful, but only partially so. He is certainly an improvement on the sluggard portrayed in the former case, a man who would not get out of his bed in the morning, but would procrastinate. You remember how he mumbled to himself: "A little more sleep, a little more slumber, a little folding of the hands to sleep."

The man portrayed in Proverbs 12 does have enough ambition to rise from his bed in the morning and go out hunting. Having caught his quarry and brought it home to dinner, however, he, too, lapses into laziness. His energy seems to desert him. He cannot be bothered to take pains to prepare his catch for dinner. He has caught it, and that is enough for one day. The thought of dressing, roasting, and then carving it is a little too much. "The slothful man roasteth not that which he took in hunting." So he resumes his former stance and lies down to sleep again.

This character is no stranger to religion. He begins with a great flurry of excitement and enthusiasm; no sacrifice is too much, and no burden too heavy. But wait a little.

The people of the coal-mining valleys of Wales have an expression: "tân siafins." It is the fire of wood chips! Such a fire blazes brightly for a couple of minutes and then dies down in as short a time as the bright flame lasted. It is totally unlike the fire made by anthracite coal, with which you have a slow start, but then a continuous blaze that lasts throughout the night.

Many Christians belong to the "wood chip" category. They have plenty of initial enthusiasm, but they are sadly deficient in the grace of perseverance. When the early excitement is gone and the early flush of enthusiasm is over, they lack the necessary resources to meet the challenge of drudgery and monotony that invariably follows. By so dropping out they fail the test of Scripture: "He that endureth to the end shall be saved" (Matthew 10:22b).

At no time has God decreed that exciting and supercharged emotional experiences are essential for Christian growth. As a matter of fact, Christians grow equally well—frequently better—without such experiences. They can make rapid progress in quiet and calm situations; and what is more, in dull and depressing situations! Situations that demand perseverance have proved to be fertile soil for Christian growth. Christians have discovered that God meets them as readily in the depths of drudgery as in the heights of rapture.

The people who constantly depend on exciting experiences—foot stomping, hand raising, tingling emotions, and rapturous ravings—are usually the ones who do not make the grade or last the race. Like King Saul of Israel, they begin their spiritual careers with fanfare and flourish, but end in depression and despair on the slopes of Mt. Gilboa. Or they are like Demas, once a beloved brother and fellow laborer of the apostle Paul, but who went out of sacred history with the sad epitaph: "Demas hath forsaken me, having loved this present world" (2 Timothy 4:10). These are the people who failed to persevere.

FATAL SLOTH

A slothful man hideth his hand in his bosom, and will not so much as bring it to his mouth again (Proverbs 19:24).

This is fatal sloth. In this instance sloth has assumed the character of a stroke or seizure. The sluggard acts as if he has lost the use of his hand, so that he cannot feed himself. He seems unable to bring the food to his mouth. It is not a case that he *cannot*, however, but that he *will not*. Rather than put forth the minimal exertion needed to feed himself, he prefers to go hungry.

This is a far more frequent occurrence in the spiritual realm than in the natural. Very few men would deny themselves physical food. However lazy a man might be, he will manage to get the food to his mouth. He has enough energy for that. But as for spiritual food, provided so lavishly by God, there are millions who deliberately go hungry for the simple reason that they cannot be bothered to exert themselves. They go for the superficial, the emotional, and the entertaining. They flock to the chorus, the film, and the sermonette. But mention the discipline of prayer, the deep study of the Word, or the rigors of witnessing, and their excitement evaporates in a hurry.

How different are the true saints. David Livingstone found enough time to read his Bible through four times each year in spite of the ceaseless traveling and exploring in his medical and missionary activity. John Wesley accomplished a herculean task on six hours sleep per night. He normally retired at 10:00 P.M. and was up again at 4:00 A.M. Wesley was indulgent compared with his friend John Fletcher of Madeley. Fletcher had so trained himself that he slept only when he could not keep awake! He prayed and meditated through two whole nights of every week. And what of old John Preston, the Puritan? He so begrudged the hours he had to sleep that "he would let the bed clothes hang down, that in the night they might fall off, and so the cold awaken him." To these men, indolence had only one meaning: it was sin.

At the Judgment Seat of Christ, the Christian will be accountable not only for the stewardship of his talent and treasure, but for the stewardship of his time as well—especially the time he wasted, the time that saw no fruit because it saw no effort. How futile in the coming day for a man to say: "But I was too involved with other things. I was too busy. I had no time."

Dr. Adams heard these excuses from his church members once too often. One Sunday morning he challenged them with this probing question: "If I were a multimillionaire and I came to your house, or your office or your study, and I said to you, 'You have some talents that are desperately important to me; will you from now until the first of the year give me five hours a week—that's all. I need those five hours a week of your time. If you will give them to me each week, I will pay you $100,000.' Would you find the five hours? Surely you wouldn't do for $100,000 something you didn't have time to do for God!"

RATIONALIZING SLOTH

> The sluggard will not plow by reason of the cold; therefore shall he beg in harvest, and have nothing (Proverbs 20:4).

Here we meet the slothful man who tries to be rational. This sluggard is not content with being merely indolent; he will go a step further and try to justify his actions. He produces reasons to explain why he should act thus. He will not plow "by reason of the cold." It sounds so much better when he can indulge in rationalizing his inactivity. Like the young lawyer who came to Jesus, he was anxious "to justify himself" (Luke 10:29). But all his justifying and rationalizing get him nowhere. When harvesttime comes, he has to go begging for bread, and he then finds that the people will not respond to him. "Therefore shall he beg in harvest, and have nothing." This fellow knew the situation only too well. When it was time to plow, he blamed the cold; but his neighbors had to plow in spite of the cold. Cold or no cold, they were out there in the fields. You can imagine how they felt toward this sluggard who had been too lazy to plow with them. Try as they would, they were never able to arouse him from his bed. Now at harvesttime they have nothing but contempt for him. Let him beg and plead, let him parade all the tear-jerking stories he can muster; they will not listen to him nor share a single crumb with him. He has to return home empty-handed, "and have nothing."

Some will no doubt react at this point and say that his fellow men should have helped him in any case, even in spite of himself. If *he* was lacking in industry, were *they* not lacking in charity? They were not a whit more lacking than the apostle Paul when he told some lazy layabouts in Thessalonica that "if any would not work, neither should he eat" (2 Thessalonians 3:10). That is a policy guaranteed to stop welfare chiseling!

To avoid misunderstanding, one should add at this point that the injunction of Paul does not apply to those who are incapable of work, nor to those who are unable to find work. Paul was not referring to such people, but to sluggards, people who do not want to work and who do nothing to look for work. Those are the people who at the end time will get their just deserts "and have nothing."

All this can be applied with equal validity to our spiritual conduct. Christians who never exert themselves, who never strive for the faith, and who never take the least risk for God—they will be found wanting in the time of harvest. Plowing and sowing are not only ministries of industry, but also ministries of faith. Where faith is concerned, there is an element of risk; there is never faith without risk. At the same time, there is no reward without risk, either. Risks bring returns, and the greater the risks, the greater the returns.

Too many Christians today have lost sight of this element of meaning in the word *faith*. They have equated faith with immunity, and by so doing have taken away its most glorious ingredient, risk. Nothing would be more rewarding than a return to a true life of faith, a life characterized by adventure, hazard, and risk. Only such a return would restore to us a heroic brand of Christianity.

> A right good thing is prudence
> And they are useful friends
> Who never make beginnings,
> Until they see the end.
> But give me now and then a man
> And I will make him king
> Who will dare to take the consequence
> And go and do the thing.

FINAL SLOTH

> I went by the field of the slothful, and by the vineyard of the man void of understanding; and, lo, it was all grown over with thorns, and nettles had covered the face thereof, and the stone wall thereof was broken down. Then I saw, and considered it well: I looked upon it, and received instruction. Yet a little sleep, a little slumber, a little folding of the hands to sleep: so shall thy poverty come as one that travelleth; and thy want as an armed man (Proverbs 24:30-34).

Here we come to the final picture of the slothful. The sun has reached its zenith, it is noon, and the sluggard is still stretched on his bed. He seems to say: "Why get involved in the rat race? Relax, take it easy, have a nap." He has said it so often that life has become one continuous siesta. "Yet a little sleep, a little slumber, a little folding of the hands to sleep."

Then Solomon, with bold strokes of the brush, painted the final picture. It was that of the sluggard's vineyard. The vineyard is fruitless. Not only that, but it is also overgrown with thorns and nettles. What is more, the stone wall is broken down. Some industrious hand had at one time planted that vineyard and erected the stone wall that protected it. But now, thanks to the sluggard, the wall is broken down and the vineyard is exposed to all intruders. Men and animals come and go at will—there is no protection. The vineyard that once was cultivated to produce fruit for the owner's household is now a rubble of stones and a breeding ground for thorns and nettles.

The ultimate evil of slothfulness is finally laid bare. It is exposed not only in its neglect of the good, but also in its encouragement of evil. "While men slept, his enemy came and sowed tares among the wheat" (Matthew 13:25). Sloth results not only in a barren vineyard, but in a vineyard taken over by the enemy.

Goodness, like a fruit tree, has to be cultivated. Badness, like a weed, grows of its own accord. In the words of William Gurnall: "This is the difference between religion and atheism, religion doth not grow without planting, but will die even where it is planted without watering. Atheism, irreligion, and profaneness are weeds that will grow without setting, but they will not die without plucking up."

What a sad end to the sluggard. His farm has been taken over by the accursed forces of nature: thorns, weeds, and nettles. The sluggard had made no exertion to plant and cultivate crops; now it is too late. He can use all the arguments he will; there is no substitute for work, and no excuse for sloth.

The sad end of the sluggard reminds me of the

story of a certain farmer in Georgia. He, too, lived in a dilapidated shack, with his farm around him neglected and forsaken. Like the farm portrayed by Solomon, weeds and nettles had taken over. Nothing had been sown, and nothing cultivated. So the Georgia farmer just sat there, ragged and barefooted, surrounded by all the evidence of his indolence.

A stranger stopped for a drink of water and in their conversation asked the farmer: "How is your cotton coming on?"

"Ain't got none," replied the farmer.

"Did you plant any?" asked the stranger.

"Nope," was the reply. "'Fraid o' boll weevils."

"Well," continued the visitor, "how is your corn?"

"Didn't plant none," came the answer. "'Fraid there wa'n't goin' to be no rain."

The visitor persevered. "Well, how are your potatoes?"

"Ain't got none; scairt o' potato bugs."

"Really, what did you plant?" pressed the stranger.

"Nothin'," was the reply. "I jest played safe."

He who never takes risks for God and never hazards his life in acts of faith will reap only the rewards of the sluggard. No risks; no returns.

Proverbs 25:21-22
If thine enemy be hungry,
give him bread to eat;
and if he be thirsty,
give him water to drink:
for thou shalt heap coals of fire upon his head,
and the LORD shall reward thee.

11

THE HIGHER GROUND—CAN I MAKE IT?

There is a "higher ground" to the life of faith. Poets have sung about it, and saints have eulogized its glories, but very few seem to have actually attained it; so few in fact, that some have questioned whether it is attainable at all. Maybe, for a few dedicated souls; but as for the ordinary, run-of-the-mill Christians, it seems way beyond reach.

Solomon, however, had no hesitation at all in answering the chapter-opening question in the affirmative. He was so sure of the matter that he took it for granted. As far as he was concerned, the higher ground to faith is well within the scope of attainability.

Unaware of the context of Solomon's statement in Proverbs 25, one would surmise that it is one of the lofty utterances of the New Testament. It refers to the higher ground of faith; to the "more excellent way" that the saints have trod. These words in Proverbs 25 stand on a par with some of the noblest statements of the Sermon on the Mount, statements like: "But I say unto you, Love your enemies, bless them that curse you, do good to them that hate you, and pray for them

143

which despitefully use you, and persecute you"
(Matthew 5:44). And they compare with statements of
the apostle Paul, like the one found in 1 Corinthians
4:12-13: "Being reviled, we bless; being persecuted,
we suffer it: being defamed, we intreat." But these
words are first found not in the gospels of the New
Testament, nor in the epistles of Paul, but way back in
the proverbs of Solomon. Joseph Parker well remarked
that "Once more we come upon the Gospel before the
time."

The presence of these words in the book of Proverbs is another proof that there is no real dichotomy
between the Old and New Testaments. Both testaments were dictated by the same Spirit, and bear the
stamp of the same author. Some have suggested that
the Old Testament revelation of God is totally different from that of the New Testament; it has even been
suggested that the Old Testament God has very little
in common with the God we meet in Jesus Christ.
That is a wrong deduction, and it denies the unity that
the Scriptures claim. The New Testament revelation is
fuller and more complete than that of the Old Testament, but it is not contradictory to it. The new commandment is simply the old commandment "which
ye had from the beginning" (1 John 2:7). It is new only
in the sense that it is enforced by a new principle and
given a new example. As for its source and authority,
they are old—even from the beginning. Here then, in
our text, is a perfect example of the unity of the Bible.
Solomon and Paul are saying the same thing. That
should not be the least bit surprising, since both were
inspired by the same Spirit. That is why the law of
love is expounded in as lofty and spiritual a manner
in the Old Testament as it is in the New. Charles
Bridges offers a salutary reminder when he says, "To
suppose that the gospel stretches beyond the measure

of the law, would imply, either that the law demanded
too little or the Gospel too much."

IDEALIZED BUT NOT REALIZED?

As already suggested, the one major criticism
brought against the wisdom of Solomon in Proverbs
25:21-22 has to do with its practicality. To love an
enemy, to feed and keep him, is undoubtedly a high
and noble counsel of perfection, but whether it can be
attained in reality is another matter. Many believe the
proverb is only an ideal that is never realized. They
believe that one might as well ask the tide not to flow,
or the sun not to shine, as to ask men of flesh and
blood to attain to this sublime standard—angels,
maybe, but men, never. It is injunctions of this kind,
we are told, that have earned Christianity the reputation of being irrelevant and impractical, and many a
Christian the criticism that he was too heavenly
minded to be of any earthly use! Yet the practicality of
these words is the very thing that matters, and the
very reason they were penned. The world is replete
with unattainable goals and ideals, but this is not one
of them. This injunction has only one purpose—to be
acted upon. It is not an abstract, unattainable ideal,
but a present, practical reality. It is for here and now.
Moreover, it is for men of flesh and blood, but flesh
and blood under the control of the divine Spirit.

DEALING WITH AN ENEMY

Solomon's words reveal the highest possible
demonstration of the Christian faith at work and un-
derscore its distinctive feature: namely, how a Christian deals with his enemy. Nothing distinguishes a
saint of God more readily than the way he puts this
injunction into effect: "If thine enemy be hungry, give
him bread to eat; and if he be thirsty, give him water
to drink."

As we saw in the last chapter, we can learn spiritual lessons from the animal kingdom, and the Bible often holds it up to us as an example. "The ox knoweth his owner, and the ass his master's crib" (Isaiah 1:3). "Go to the ant, thou sluggard; consider her ways, and be wise" (Proverbs 6:6). But one looks in vain to the animal kingdom for an example of the kind of behavior Solomon advocates in Proverbs 25:21-22. Where in the animal kingdom does one find love exchanged for hate, and kindness for hostility? Maybe the closest we come to it is found in an illustration from Sir Walter Scott. He told of the occasion when he was taught an invaluable lesson by a stray dog. This dog bothered him intensely; so out of desperation he picked up a stone and threw it at him. His intention was to frighten the dog away, but unfortunately, he threw the stone harder and straighter than he had planned. The stone hit the dog and broke its leg; but instead of becoming vicious or running away, the dog limped up to Sir Walter and licked his hand. The great writer never forgot that experience. He had never expected such a reaction from a stray dog.

Such a reaction, says the Bible, should be the norm for the sanctified believer. Returning good for evil, love for hate, and kindness for vengeance is the higher ground that he is told to attain and enabled to attain by the aid of God's Spirit within.

To help us make use of this counsel of wisdom, let us consider three things about it.

It proceeds from God the Father. From whom else could such perfection of love come! In most systems of ethics the Golden Rule seems to be the highest standard proclaimed, the highest goal for men to reach: do unto others as you would have them do unto you. Even this standard is too high for some people. About the only standard they can attain is that of the rabbinical school of the Pharisees in Israel: "Thou shalt love thy neighbor and hate thine enemy." That is the standard that appeals most to human nature and is most attainable by human nature, but it was not the standard proclaimed by God for His people. What the Pharisees had done was to cover many of the original injunctions of the Old Testament with a layer of their own traditions, presumably at first to protect the original. But in time the process only succeeded in perverting the original. Let us look at one example. Back in the book of Exodus, Moses had proclaimed in terminology appropriate to his day, "If thou meet thine enemy's ox or his ass going astray, thou shalt surely bring it back to him again" (Exodus 23:4). So the vital truth was already there in the Law of Moses, but unfortunately, it had become buried under many coatings of rabbinical traditions. In the book of Proverbs, however, and in the gospels and epistles of the New Testament, this truth becomes visible again, budding and blossoming forth into full life. We see it in Proverbs 25:21-22; in Romans 12:19-21; and in Matthew 5:44-45. Chronologically, we can trace back this precious line: Paul, Jesus, Solomon, Moses. But remember, the teaching did not originate even with Moses. Moses' version was only a carbon copy. The original is found deep in the heart and character of God.

We know this to be true because we know how God deals with His own enemies. Indeed, it is the way He dealt with us when we were His enemies. Man became God's enemy in Adam, and the same enmity has characterized every man since Adam. The whole human race is guilty of rebellion against its Maker, of worshiping the creature rather than the Creator. As God looked down upon the earth, He declared it to be corrupt. In spite of that, God decided He would visit

His enemies, not with the intention of destroying them, but with a desire to redeem them. This is the good news of the gospel: "Blessed be the Lord God of Israel; for he hath visited and redeemed his people" (Luke 1:68). He came to give eyes to the blind, feet to the lame, health to the diseased; yes, and pardon to the guilty, salvation to the sinner, and love to the enemy. When we are asked to love our enemies, we are only asked to imitate what God has already done. Paul spells it out in Romans 5:10. "When we were enemies, we were reconciled to God by the death of his Son."

This law, of course, is in no sense native to this planet, or to man. It is a law that comes direct from heaven and the heart of God.

It is exemplified in God the Son. Other examples of loving your enemies could be found, but they lack the completeness and perfection one finds in Christ. One example we could profitably look at, however, is that of the prophet Elisha, and how he dealt with the army of Syria. Syria's army had been sent to capture the prophet and take him back to Syria as a prisoner. When they surrounded the little town of Dothan and his capture seemed inevitable, the prophet called upon God. As a result of that prayer, the Syrian army was struck with blindness. Instead of capturing Elisha, they themselves were captured and placed at the mercy of the king of Israel. It is obvious that the king's intention was to put his enemies to the sword, and this was his great opportunity. But before he could exercise his vengeance upon them, Elisha intervened on their behalf. He informed the king of the more excellent way and counseled him accordingly. "Set bread and water before them, that they may eat and drink, and go to their master" (2 Kings 6:22). Let it be said to the king's credit that he acted upon the

prophet's advice. Here then was a real-life demonstration of the truth of Solomon, one that was enacted
back in Old Testament days. Elisha did the very thing
that Solomon wrote about. He fed his enemies, satisfied their hunger, and quenched their thirst. No wonder Bishop Hall cried out: "O noble revenge of Elisha
to feast his persecutors! To provide a table for those
who had provided a grave for him!" This is the only
kind of revenge a Christian is allowed—the revenge
that feeds an enemy.

Concerning this matter of revenge, Dr. R. G. Lee
illustrated it very aptly when he said that the lower
you go in the scale of being, the more you find the
spirit of revenge. Go down from man, and you come at
length to the hornet and the rattlesnake. You hurt
them; they hurt you. But go up from man to angels
and archangels and you come to the throne of God.
What do you find there? Revenge and resentment? No.
What you find there is love, boundless and immeasur-
able.

In the person and life of Jesus one finds this love
being demonstrated upon earth in all the perfection of
its heavenly quality. Jesus was wounded by our in-
human behavior, and yet He continued to love us. He
was bruised and battered, but continued to love;
falsely accused, shamefully betrayed, and callously
denied, but He loved on; whipped and scourged, yet
He loved on. The rabble taunted Him, the soldiers spat
on Him, the political figures mocked Him, the religious leaders scorned Him, but He loved on. In spite of
the thorns, the nails, the cross itself—the vilest and
cruelest of all deaths—He still loved on. His words
ring down the ages: "Father, forgive them; for they
know not what they do" (Luke 23:34). In that hour He
exemplified the more excellent way as no one has ever
done before or after. The injunction given by God

from heaven found its complete fulfillment on earth in Jesus. He loved His enemies, blessed them that cursed Him, and did good to those that despitefully used Him.

It is fulfilled in the power of God the Holy Spirit. It is not within man's capacity to fulfill this injunction to love your enemies; it can only be fulfilled by the power of the Holy Spirit working within him. Man is unable to believe the truths of the gospel, let alone practice them, unless he is enabled to do so by the Holy Spirit.

Mary, the mother of Jesus, could not understand the truth of the virgin birth. "How shall this be?" was her question. The archangel answered: "The Holy Ghost" (Luke 1:34-35).

Nicodemus, although a leader in Israel, could not understand the truth of rebirth. He asked, "How can a man be born when he is old?" Jesus answered: "Of the Spirit" (John 3:4-5).

The crowds that gathered on the streets of Jerusalem on the day of Pentecost could not understand the strange behavior of the apostles. Were they intoxicated with new wine? "What meaneth this?" they asked. Peter gave the same answer: it was the Holy Spirit (Acts 2:12-18).

It is only by the power of the Holy Spirit that a man can understand the truths of the gospel, and it is only by the power of the Holy Spirit that a man can accept the truths of the gospel. "No man can say that Jesus is the Lord, but by the Holy Ghost" (1 Corinthians 12:3). We can proceed and say that it is only by the same Holy Spirit that a man can obey the injunctions of the gospel. It is only in the Spirit's power that these seemingly impossible injunctions can be obeyed, and these otherwise unattainable standards realized. It is

God the Holy Spirit working within us. He alone can transform ideals into reality.

LOVE: HUMAN AND DIVINE

Human love can extend only to that which is lovable. Men love someone or something because of a quality in the object that awakens and responds to their love. In other words, the object must possess the quality to be loved. This is why men love purity, beauty, and perfection—for the simple reason that they are lovable. It is impossible to love the unlovable. We love the rose but not the thorn. Such is human love.

How different is the divine love implanted in us by the Holy Spirit. Divine love operates not because of any worth or quality in the object, but because of something in the one doing the loving.

Where can there be a more perfect example of divine love than in the death of God's own Son on Calvary. When He loved man, He loved not the good, the pure, and the perfect; but rather the bad, the impure, and the imperfect—not the just and the righteous, but the unjust and the unrighteous. How could He do this? How could a thrice-holy God, too holy even to behold iniquity, manage to love such a disreputable creature as man? How could He condescend to love the most stained and sordid inhabitants of earth? It was not because of anything in them, but because of something in Him. "Behold, what manner of love the Father hath bestowed upon us, that we should be called the sons of God" (1 John 3:1).

How was George Whitefield able to love those malevolent critics who heaped their slander and abuse upon him? William Cowper tells us:

> He loved the world that hated him.
> The tear that fell upon his Bible was sincere.
> Assailed by scandal and the tongue of strife,
> His only answer was a blameless life.

How could Whitefield react in that way? It was nothing in them; but something in him.

How could one of those unnamed and unsung saints of Russia respond so divinely to his persecutors? One of those persecutors testified and stated that when they spat in the Christian's face, he looked up to heaven and praised God for the dew! It was nothing in them, but something in him.

How could Paul tell the Corinthians: "Being reviled, we bless; being persecuted, we suffer it: being defamed, we intreat" (1 Corinthians 4:12-13). Receiving a curse, Paul returned a blessing. How could he react so magnanimously to his worst enemies? It was nothing in them, but something in him.

It was the same with Stephen, the man who imitated his Lord so closely. He prayed for the ones who were brutally stoning him to death. Even as his frail body was being mangled into pulp, he was able to pray with his ebbing breath, "Lord, lay not this sin to their charge" (Acts 7:60). Again we ask: how could frail human spirit respond like that? It was nothing in them, but something in him.

There have been countless other Christians to this day who have gone forth to fulfill the same injunction. They march in the vanguard of the saints when they love their enemies and bless their foes. This is the highest standard of behavior that mankind can ever witness, the highest ground that mortal man can ever attain. This is the more excellent way of which the Bible speaks. And the ones who attain it do so because they are privy to the grand secret: by His Spirit we conquer.

THE TWO PROMISES

The man who fulfills the injunction to love your enemies is given two promises by God. *He will see an enemy become a friend.* Some people have stumbled at the phrase in Proverbs 25:22, "for thou shalt heap coals of fire upon his head." After the perfect love depicted in verse 21, many think this statement in verse 22 falls short of the goal. It seems to revert to normal, human love. They argue that if the motive behind feeding an enemy is to heap coals of fire upon his head, then it is not love at all, but a subtle and sophisticated form of revenge.

That is an inaccurate deduction for the simple reason that it is based on a misunderstanding of the "Orientalism" of the expression. In no way should the figure "heap coals of fire" be interpreted as torture of one's enemy. As a matter of fact, it is the very opposite.

In the East, almost everything is carried on the head: waterpots, baskets of fruit—even braziers of fire. In many of the homes, the only fire the people have is that kept in the brazier, and it is used for both cooking and warmth. Normally, such a fire is never allowed to go out, but in the unhappy event that it does, the woman of the house will then go and borrow fire from her neighbor, with the brazier on her head. If her neighbor happens to be an exceptionally generous woman, she will not only lend her fire, but she will heap some coals on the fire as well. Such a neighbor obviously walks the second mile. She is not only generous, but "generous-plus."

In the same way, says Solomon, when you feed an enemy and quench his thirst, it is like heaping coals of fire on his head. You are multiplying goodness to him; compounding kindness; going way beyond the letter of the law. Such an act on your part will convict an enemy as no word of yours ever could. Keep on heaping the coals and you will have no problem getting his attention; no problem witnessing to him about the salvation of his soul; no problem getting him to church; and no problem directing his enmity into friendship. By such an action, Jesus taught, "thou hast gained thy brother" (Matthew 18:15).

Abraham Lincoln is said to have attended a banquet in Washington when America was experiencing deep trouble with the South. During the banquet he dropped a kindly remark in favor of the southerners. All at once, a woman flared up and rebuked him: "Destroy your enemies."

Lincoln came back with an answer worthy of the saints: "Madam, do I not destroy my enemies when I make them my friends?"

He will himself be rewarded by God. Not only is he who loves his enemy rewarded by seeing an enemy become a friend, but he will be personally rewarded as well by God. "And the LORD shall reward thee" (Proverbs 25:22b).

God has a secret method by which He recompenses His saints: He sees to it that they become the prime beneficiaries of their own benefactions! Such a method may make no sense in the hard world of commerce and business, but it is the method by which God works. God ensures that the one who gives is the one who gets. The one who loses his life is the one who saves his life. The one who feeds an enemy is the one who wins an enemy. All that, and still there is something more: God will also reward him in the coming day.

NOTES

Chapter 1
1. Henry Thomas and Dana L. Thomas, *Living Biographies of Famous Rulers* (Garden City, N.Y.: Blue Ribbon, 1946), pp. 4-5, 7-8.
2. Alexander Whyte, *Bible Characters*, 2 vols. (London: Oliphants, 1952), 1:278.

Chapter 4
1. Upton Sinclair, *The Cup of Fury* (Great Neck, N.Y.: Channel, 1956), pp. 14, 18.

Chapter 5
1. Paul E. Larsen, *Wise Up and Live* (Glendale, Cal.: Regal, 1974), p. 124.

Chapter 6
1. C. S. Lovett, *What's a Parent to Do?* (Baldwin Park, Cal.: Personal Christianity, 1971), pp. 17-18.

Chapter 7
1. D. James Kennedy, *The God of Great Surprises* (Wheaton, Ill.: Tyndale, 1973), p. 33.
2. Helen Waddell, trans., *The Desert Fathers* (New York: Barnes & Noble, 1936), pp. 267-81.

Chapter 8
1. Robert Flood, *America God Shed His Grace on Thee* (Chicago: Moody, 1975), p. 174.

Moody Press, a ministry of the Moody Bible Institute, is designed for education, evangelization, and edification. If we may assist you in knowing more about Christ and the Christian life, please write us without obligation: Moody Press, c/o MLM, Chicago, Illinois 60610.